C000079079

How to teach non-fiction writing at key stage 3

DRAGON SCHOOL
OXFORD

WRITERS' WORKSHOP SERIES

How to teach non-fiction writing at key stage 3

PAUL EVANS

David Fulton Publishers
London

David Fulton Publishers Ltd
414 Chiswick High Road, London W4 5TF

www.fultonpublishers.co.uk

First published in Great Britain in 2002 by David Fulton Publishers
Reprinted 2003
10 9 8 7 6 5 4 3 2

Note: the right of Paul Evans to be identified as the author of this work has been asserted by him in accordance with the Copyright, Design and Patents Act 1998

Copyright © Paul Evans 2002

British Library Cataloguing in Publication Data
A catalogue record for this book is available from the British Library.

ISBN 1-85346-859-2

The materials in this publication may be photocopied only for use within the purchasing organisation. Otherwise, all rights reserved. No part of this publication may be reproduced, stored in a retrieval system, or transmitted, in any form or by any means, electronic, mechanical, photocopying, or otherwise, without the prior permission of the publishers.

Also available in the **Writers' Workshop Series:**
How to teach writing across the curriculum at key stage 2   *Sue Palmer*   ISBN 1-85346-803-7
How to teach poetry writing at key stage 2   *Michaela Morgan*   ISBN 1-85346-804-5
How to teach fiction writing at key stage 2   *Pie Corbett*   ISBN 1-85346-833-9

Forthcoming:

How to teach fiction writing at key stage 3   *Neil MacRae*   ISBN 1-85346-858-4
How to teach poetry writing at key stage 3   *Pie Corbett*   ISBN 1-85346-915-7

Page design by Ken Vail Graphic Design
Typeset by FiSH Books, London
Printed and bound in Great Britain by Thanet Press Limited, Margate, Kent.

Contents

Acknowledgements

The publishers would like to thank the staff and pupils of Lipson Community College for their help with the cover photographs.

Thanks are due to the following copyright holders for permission to reproduce materials in this book:

J. S. Jones, for the extract from *Almost Like a Whale*, published by Transworld Publishers, a division of the Random House Group Ltd. All rights reserved. © J. S. Jones 1999.

Matthew Parris and *The Spectator* for 'Eating our fellow-mammals may not be wrong, but it is not very nice', first published in *The Spectator*, 21 April 2001.

News International Newspapers Ltd, for '$130,000 for a glob of ketchup', by Paul Thomson, © *The Sun*, 28 May 2001.

Philip Hensher and Independent Newspapers Ltd for 'Harry Potter – give me a break', first published in *The Independent*, 25 January 2000.

Penguin Books Ltd, for the extract from *Citizens*, by Simon Schama, © Penguin 1989.

The Random House Group Ltd for the extract from *Experience* by Martin Amis, published by Jonathan Cape, 2000. Reprinted by permission.

Introduction

The link between reading and writing

The teaching and learning promoted by this book establish a clear link between reading and writing.

We are encouraging pupils to read analytically, to identify the key features of texts at word, sentence and text levels, and then to use that analysis so that they can use the identified features in their own writing.

Key features of a text

So, what might the key features of a text at word, sentence and text level be?

Features of texts at word level

- vocabulary
- use of specialised/technical words
- stock words and phrases
- use of obscure words
- recurrence of certain words
- imagery
- words that betray opinion/prejudice
- experimentation with words
- words that help to create an impersonal/formal text
- use of rhythm/rhyme/alliteration/assonance

Features of texts at sentence level

- use of simple/compound/complex sentences
- use of conjunctions and connectives
- length of sentences
- structure of sentences
- punctuation
- analysis of word classes predominantly used
- punctuation
- tense
- active/passive voice
- 1st/2nd/3rd person
- paragraphing
- links between paragraphs

Features of texts at text level

- audience
- purpose
- form
- structure
- sequence
- author's intentions
- themes
- issues
- design
- layout
- use of illustrations

DRAGON SCHOOL
OXFORD

Once the key features have been identified, a further crucial question must be addressed. What is the effect on the reader of the use of that feature? Or to put the question another way: what was the author's purpose in using that particular feature?

In response to this question, two answers are banned:

- to make the text more interesting;
- to make the reader want to read on.

These answers are not banned because they are wrong, but because they are *always* right. When we probe deeper into the 'effect question' it becomes a much more interesting one, and one which gives rise to many possible answers.

As an example, look at Task 2 in 'Investigating persuasion texts' (p. 63). The question 'Why are dashes used in text?' could trigger a range of responses beyond the one suggested on Grid 2. All reasonable answers can be accepted as correct. Pupils will begin to understand that there are often no hard and fast answers to the 'effect question', will become happier with that uncertainty, will be able to talk and write about it with growing confidence, and will be able to produce more and more sophisticated responses, of the kind that gain higher marks in examinations. The pupil who can think, then say, then write 'On the one hand, this could imply... On the other, it could be said that...' is well on the way to high levels of achievement, both in English and in many other subjects.

The above argument can be summarised clearly for pupils, as in Figure 1.

The teaching sequence

A clear teaching sequence backs up the link between reading and writing, and can raise pupils' attainment levels in both activities.

Establish clear aims

Tell pupils why they are reading this particular text and how the reading of the text will lead, perhaps over a series of lessons, to their own writing of a similar text.

Establish clear outcomes

Make sure that pupils understand what success will look like at the end of this lesson and at the end of the sequence of lessons. There must be opportunities for pupils to demonstrate in every lesson that they have learned something. They need to be given opportunities to celebrate their learning and to articulate exactly what the learning is and how they achieved it.

Read for meaning

Pupils can be helped to read challenging texts through the use of active reading strategies, including:

- teaching a clear distinction between *skimming* (reading quickly for gist), *scanning* (looking for a specific piece of information) and *close reading* (word by word);
- reading aloud by the teacher, by individual pupils, by groups and by the whole class;
- marking texts in response to focused questions, such as 'Find out the three most important things about the religious beliefs of the Romans';
- focused, time-limited discussion of texts in pairs or small groups;
- reporting back to groups or the whole class on an aspect of the text;
- transforming information gained from the text into an interview, a short play, a drawing, a diagram, etc.;
- the teacher modelling how to read a text for information, articulating the thought processes involved in reading.

Analyse features of text at word, sentence and text levels

See 'Key features of a text' above.

Discuss the effects of those features

See 'Key features of a text' above.

Teacher modelling of writing

The teacher shows pupils how to write, by:

Reading		Writing	
Identify the key features of the text at word, sentence and text levels	Describe the effects that the key features create	Decide which effects you want to create in your own text	Use the features that will create those effects

Figure 1 Establishing the link between reading and writing

- deciding what effects (s)he wants to create in the writing;
- using the appropriate features;
- talking her/his way through a short piece of writing, articulating what is going on in the head of a writer as (s)he writes;
- asking pupils at this stage simply to watch and listen, because later in the teaching and learning sequence they will be doing the same thing.

This is very difficult and takes a lot of practice. Many teachers, when they start modelling, write the sentences before the lesson, so that they can concentrate on demonstrating the decision-making process rather than having to think about the actual composition of text at the same time.

Shared writing

The teacher invites pupils to contribute their own ideas. These ideas are still fashioned by the teacher into the form in which they appear in writing. The teacher is still, then, making and articulating the decisions about composition, but pupils are being drawn into the process.

Supported composition

The teacher asks pupils, in pairs, to write a few more sentences of the text. During the composition time, the teacher walks around the room, listening to the talk between partners. (S)he is expecting to hear the kind of talk that (s)he modelled at the start of the sequence. In other words, pupils are becoming conscious of themselves as writers, and are saying things like: 'What do you think we should put at the beginning of the next paragraph to connect it to the previous one?' It is very important that pupils continue to develop 'the feel for the sentence'. They should be encouraged to speak sentences before writing them down, and to do a lot of sorting and editing before the words reach the paper. Teachers can introduce this idea in quite a regimented fashion, asking pupils to speak their next sentence to their partner or to stand up as a class and all speak their sentence out loud.

Guided writing

The teacher works with a group of pupils of similar ability in writing, while the rest of the class does scaffolded or independent writing (see below). The teacher intervenes with the group at the point of composition, eliminating errors and raising the standard of the writing. This session might also include some shared writing, where the whole group joins in the composition of one text. At this point, it might be appropriate to introduce consideration of spelling and handwriting.

Scaffolded writing

While the teacher is working on guided writing with the group, some pupils might be working without the teacher but with the support of a writing frame or a list of connectives or a compilation of points to be made or a dictionary, etc.

Independent writing

All pupils should be given regular opportunities to work independently, that is totally unaided. This is their opportunity to show what they have learned from this lesson or sequence of lessons. The session will not last long, probably no more than 20 minutes in most lessons, but is crucial to the development of self-esteem and the genuine independence that is the aim of all teaching.

Reflection

Pupils should have the opportunity, in a plenary session, to celebrate what they have learned, and to reflect on what they have learned and how they did it. Pupils should leave the room with a sense of pride in their achievements, wanting to come back for more.

This whole sequence represents a journey from total dependence on the teacher – through interdependence – to independence. Pupils should go through the whole sequence regularly.

Progression in sentence construction

To guide them through the writing process, pupils need to know how to make their sentences more and more flexible, better and better adapted to purpose. Figure 2 illustrates a possible model for progression that could be presented to pupils.

I can	• write in sentences. • join ideas with *and* and *then.* • choose the right word. • use capital letters and full stops sometimes in simple sentences.
I can	• write sentences that do not always start with the subject. • join ideas with *but* and *so.* • choose interesting words. • use capital letters and full stops most of the time in simple sentences.
I can	• start sentences in different ways. • use words to link ideas or events. • use descriptive words and phrases. • use correct punctuation most of the time.
I can	• use connectives like *but/when/so/because.* • use appropriate vocabulary. • use adjectives and adverbs. • write *we were,* not *we was.* • use capital letters, full stops and question marks accurately at least half of the time.
I can	• use connectives like *if/when/rather than/although/however.* • use pronouns correctly. • stick to the right tense. • use adventurous vocabulary. • use appropriate layout. • use capital letters, full stops and question marks accurately most of the time. • use commas to separate clauses, phrases and items in a list.
I can	• vary the length and structure of my sentences for effect. • use language precisely and effectively, including technical vocabulary. • decide how formal I need the language to be and stick to it. • use paragraphs. • use capital letters, full stops, question marks and commas accurately all the time. • use capital letters for proper nouns. • use brackets and dashes where appropriate.

Figure 2 Progress in sentence construction

I can	● match the style of my writing to the purpose and audience. ● use an impersonal style where appropriate. ● use a range of sentence lengths and structures, and a varied vocabulary, to create effects that match the form and purpose. ● organise my ideas into paragraphs, including introduction and summary. ● use a range of punctuation correctly, to vary pace and clarify meaning. ● use colons and semi-colons.
I can	● use a range of structures, such as adverbial phrases and impersonal openings, to vary the length and focus of sentences and to express shades of meaning. ● use connectives within and between paragraphs to show the links between my ideas. ● use topic sentences at the start of paragraphs. ● use introductions and conclusions to give direction and contribute to the effectiveness of my writing. ● use a range of punctuation to create deliberate effects. ● use dashes, bullet points and parenthetic commas.
I can	● vary sentence structure to achieve particular effects. ● use active and passive voices where appropriate. ● move between tenses appropriately. ● vary the length of paragraphs to control and develop ideas, and to create impact. ● use a range of text connectives. ● use a range of vocabulary to express shades of meaning. ● use accurate punctuation to vary pace, clarify meaning, avoid ambiguity and create deliberate effects.
I can	● use an appropriate style to secure and sustain the reader's involvement. ● develop a point of view, using a range of sophisticated ideas, with appropriate and lively illustration. ● use paragraphs to give sense of coherence and completeness. ● use vocabulary, grammar and sentence structure to develop and support complex ideas. ● use punctuation accurately, appropriately and with sensitivity to meaning.

Figure 2 continued

Text Types

The format of this book reflects the six main types of non-fiction as defined in the Year 7 teaching objectives of the National Literacy Strategy Framework. It uses a wide variety of strategies to tackle the text types and tries to avoid too much repetition of any one strategy. The strategies are mostly interchangeable: they can be used in working on any text type, not just the one with which they are linked in the book. Some tasks, and some texts, are more difficult than others. Taken together, they represent a reasonable expectation of what most pupils are expected to tackle in Key Stage 3. Lower-ability pupils are now entering secondary education with the expectation that they will deal with challenging texts and ideas. We must not disappoint them.

The Year 7 Framework also introduces the 'triplets' of purposes for writing – writing to imagine/explore/entertain, to inform/explain/describe, to persuade/argue/advise, to analyse/review/comment. This notion of writing purposes runs through the whole English curriculum at Key Stages 3 and 4 and forms the basis for the categorisation of reading and writing tasks in English GCSE. The question 'What was the author's purpose in this text?' also relates very closely to the central issue of effect, as discussed above.

In these circumstances, the issue of purpose can never be ignored, and is specifically addressed in the book, particularly in relation to information texts. Looking at the extract from Steve Jones's book *Almost Like a Whale*, for example (p. 24), pupils come to realise that there can be many different purposes underlying one text. Jones is not simply writing to give us, his readers, pure information. So, what are his other purposes? What is he actually trying to do to us? As always with effect questions, there are many possible answers. The debate that is thereby raised can broaden and deepen pupils' understanding of how non-fiction texts work. At Key Stage 2, pupils have been taught to categorise non-fiction texts fairly rigidly into the main text types, as defined by the primary National Literacy Framework. At Key Stage 3, part of our job is to blow those categories apart to some extent, to show pupils that most texts cross those boundaries and aim to achieve many different purposes at once.

There is also scope for playing with text types. Pupils can be given opportunities to demonstrate their understanding both of the content of the material they are handling and of the conventions of text types by transforming texts from one type to another. For example:

- write a newspaper interview with the widow of the wolf from 'Little Red Riding Hood';
- turn the making of the monster in 'Frankenstein' into an account of a scientific experiment;
- write a recipe as an autobiography:

    As I walked into the kitchen on that blazing summer's morning, I knew that I needed something to calm the rage that was still boiling inside me from the revelations of the night before...

- re-write a travel brochure as a truthful account of a visit to the resort in question.

Pupils should also be encouraged to carry out investigations of texts, for example:

- *After four years of marriage, Janice and Adrian Smith seemed happy together, living comfortably in their new semi in suburbia. Janice, 22, looked after the home, while her husband worked nights at a canning factory. All that was missing was the child they had been trying to conceive for the last two years.*
    What kind of text is it? How do you know? At what point do you know it is non-fiction? If you gave it to pupils sentence by sentence, would their perceptions change twice? What kind of publication does it come from? How do you know?
- Look at the language of young children as they learn to speak. Why does a young child say a word like 'goed' when it has never heard anyone else say it? Which word class usually comes first in speech? (Noun.) Which comes second? (Verb.) What does this tell us about sentence construction? (That sentences are constructed around nouns and verbs.)
- Investigate the nature of jokes, clichés, pop songs, slang, dialect.
- Think of 100 ways of saying 'Go away' or some other familiar utterance. What influences the degree of politeness/formality that you use?
- Investigate the kind of language associated with specific places or situations, e.g. the Headteacher's room, school reports, etc.
- Investigate a transcript of speech and examine the differences between talking and writing, e.g.
    there was a big – loud – not a – like – not an explosion like you hear in films or anything – you know a big bang – but I – at first I didn't hear – well anything really – because I had my – music – Walkman – on

- Investigate new words and new meanings, e.g. *nerd, freak, bad, naff.*
- Collect examples of formal language, e.g. application forms, credit agreements, birth, marriage and death ceremonies. Analyse them at word, sentence and text levels. Imitate them. Re-write them in more accessible language.
- Collect examples of 'incorrect' usage. What is wrong with them? Does it matter? Is 'wrong' the wrong word?

The writing journal

We want to encourage our pupils to see reading and writing as two halves of the same learning process.

Just as we want them to experience the joy of reading, so we want them to find joy in writing. We want them to carry a reading book in one pocket and a writing journal in the other. Inside the journal, we might find:

- Pupils' reflections on anything at all, written down at random in odd moments;
- Pieces of unstructured writing that we have encouraged them to do at specified times in English lessons. When a teacher first says that the class will have 15 minutes each fortnight when they can write about anything they like, the reaction is bafflement. No other objectives?

We can't write without objectives! Within three weeks, most pupils are asking for extra time. The only rule is that you must write for the 15 minutes, not stare out of the window. The teacher will mark the writing not for spelling, punctuation, grammar or handwriting, but as one human being responding to another, sharing thoughts and experiences. The teacher might suggest to someone who writes about football every week that he might like to write about something else, but this will only be a suggestion. Interest in writing will surge forward in this classroom.

- Examples of pupils trying out the techniques to which they have been introduced in the lesson. The pieces of writing they attempt with a partner during supported composition might feature here, along with more extended drafts, and reflections on how effectively the techniques are being used.
- Pupils reflecting, as a result of the plenary, on what they have learned and how they have learned it.
- Pupils recording targets they have been given, or targets which they have set themselves, and assessments of their progress towards the targets.
- Pupils reflecting on what they have learned about writing in other subjects.

Investigating information texts

Task 1: Reading information texts

✍ Notes for teachers

- Look at Information Text 1.

  - *Allow pupils to read the text in pairs. Tell them that, in two minutes' time, you will be asking them to tell you in one phrase what it is about and also to tell you three facts that they have discovered from the text.*

- Pick out some features of the text at word, sentence and text levels. What is the purpose of the text? Who is its intended audience? Use Grid 1 to help you.

  - *You may need to model this process, marking the text and beginning to fill in the grid. An exemplar answer sheet is shown as Grid 2.*

- Now write an analysis of Text 1 in continuous prose.

  - *You will need to model this process, e.g. 'The purpose of this is to help birdwatchers identify a particular bird. I know this is the case because...'*
  - *You could divide the task up, so that each pupil or pair writes about one aspect of the analysis.*
  - *Always encourage pupils to speak their next sentence before they write it down. Let them try it out on their partners. This will help them to develop a 'feel' for sentence structure – that a sentence is not a brief phrase, nor is it a rambling attempt to say everything you know at once.*
  - *At this early stage, it might be a good idea to restrict pupils who are finding this difficult to a two-sentence formula, as shown above:*
    Sentence 1: statement, e.g. 'The purpose is...'
    Sentence 2: justification, e.g. 'I know this because...'

Task 1: Reading information texts

- Look at Information Text 1.

- Pick out some features of the text at word, sentence and text levels. What is the purpose of the text? Who is its intended audience? Use Grid 1 to help you.

- Now write an analysis of Text 1 in continuous prose.

© 2002 Paul Evans *How to Teach Non-fiction Writing at KS3* (1 85346 859 2). Published by David Fulton Publishers

BAR-TAILED LARK

Ammomanes cincturus. Smaller than Desert Lark, but with distinctive round head, shorter bill and well-defined dark bar at tip of shorter tail and blackish wing tips; and legs darker. Song weak, fluty, trisyllabic; flight call like Short-toed. Mainly in deserts with little vegetation and few rocks; often in small flocks. L 15 cm.

From *Collins Pocket Guide, Birds of Britain and Europe*, HarperCollins, reprinted 1998

Information Text 1

Text analysed:

Purpose • What is it for? • How do you know?	•
Audience • Who is it for? • How do you know?	•
Features at word level Think about: • specialised vocabulary • stock words and phrases	•
Features at sentence level Think about: • tense • length of sentences • structure of sentences • conjunctions and connectives • punctuation • 1st/2nd/3rd person • active/passive voice	•
Features at text level Think about: • layout • structure • sequence	•

Grid 1 Analysis of Information Text 1

Text analysed: *Birds of Britain*

Purpose
- What is it for?
- How do you know?

- *To help identify birds*
- *Very detailed; explains differences from related species*

Audience
- Who is it for?
- How do you know?

- *Birdwatchers*
- *Too detailed for casual admirers of birds*

Features at word level
Think about:
- specialised vocabulary
- stock words and phrases

- *Latin name*
- *Names of other kinds of lark*
- *Descriptive words, e.g. weak, fluty, well-defined*
- *Lots of adjectives add precision*
- *L 15 cm - secret language for incrowd of birdwatchers*

Features at sentence level
Think about:
- tense
- length of sentences
- structure of sentences
- conjunctions and connectives
- punctuation
- 1st/2nd/3rd person
- active/passive voice

- *No verbs at all - pure description - note form - present tense assumed*
- *3 long sentences - 1 about appearance - 1 about song - 1 about habitat*
- *Perhaps this is the pattern for all entries in the book?*
- *Facts within 3 categories separated by commas and semi-colons*
- *We'd be in trouble if we wrote like this*

Features at text level
Think about:
- layout
- structure
- sequence

- *Very compact - book filled with entries*
- *English name in bold to make it easier to find in book*
- *Sequence - appearance - song - habitat - not signposted because of lack of space*
- *Illustration would help to clarify text*

Grid 2 An exemplar answer for the analysis of Information Text 1

Task 2: Writing information texts

✍ Notes for teachers

- Look at Information Text 2.

- Carry out an analysis of its features, using Grid 3.

  - *This activity begins with a routine that is now familiar from Task 1.*

- Write a letter to the parents of pupils in your year group giving details of a weekend trip to the theatre at the end of term.

  - *You will need to make and record decisions about the following: names, dates and times; who the writer of the letter is; what the pupils will need to bring with them; how much the trip costs and what will be done to help those who cannot afford the trip.*
  - *Ask pupils to help you to devise a list such as the above and record their decisions, so that they can be kept in view throughout the lesson.*

- Look at this list of purposes for writing: to imagine; to explore; to entertain; to inform; to explain; to describe; to persuade; to argue; to advise. Which of these – as well as to inform – might you want to use in this letter? What words, phrases and sentences might you use?

  - *This activity introduces the pupils to the 'triplets' of purposes for writing, which first appear in the Year 7 objectives of the NLS Framework, and which apply all the way through Key Stages 3 and 4 to the GCSE English exam.*
  - *It also introduces them to the idea that most pieces of writing have more than one purpose. In this case, the letter might need to persuade reluctant parents to allow their children to go on the trip. It might need to entertain, i.e. to 'sell' the idea that the trip will be fun. There might be many other purposes, which pupils can identify.*

- Use Grid 4 to help you make decisions about how you will write the letter. You must stick to those decisions when you write. Some possible answers have been provided to start you off.

- When you have written your first draft, review it by looking at Grid 4, which shows what you intended to do. Have you carried out your intentions? Is the letter clear? Is it interesting? Does it tell the parents clearly what they have to do next?

  - *This process is important in developing pupils' ability to evaluate their own work. It encourages them to work to objectives, and to become independent learners.*

- When you have reviewed your first draft, pass it over to your partner for comments.

- *Pupils should never pass their work to others for comment before they have thoroughly reviewed it themselves. Asking another person to comment on your work does not mean that it ceases to be your responsibility.*
- *Response partners need to be trained to praise strengths, as well as suggesting areas for improvement. They too must be focused on objectives.*

- When you have finished the final draft, write an analysis of your letter, explaining what you were trying to do and evaluating how well you think you succeeded.

- *You may need to model this process, to encourage pupils to move beyond the bland – 'I thought I did quite well' – to the particular – 'The purpose of this sentence was to ... To achieve this purpose I used ...'*

Task 2: Writing information texts

- Look at Information Text 2.

- Carry out an analysis of its features, using Grid 3.

- Write a letter to the parents of pupils in your year group giving details of a weekend trip to the theatre at the end of term.

- Look at this list of purposes for writing: to imagine; to explore; to entertain; to explain; to describe; to persuade; to argue; to advise. Which of these – as well as to inform – might you want to use in this letter? What words, phrases and sentences might you use?

- Use Grid 4 to help you make decisions about how you will write the letter. You must stick to those decisions when you write. Some possible answers have been provided to start you off.

- When you have written your first draft, review it by looking at Grid 4, which shows what you intended to do. Have you carried out your intentions? Is the letter clear? Is it interesting? Does it tell the parents clearly what they have to do next?

- When you have reviewed your first draft, pass it over to your partner for comments.

- When you have finished the final draft, write an analysis of your letter, explaining what you were trying to do and evaluating how well you think you succeeded.

© 2002 Paul Evans *How to Teach Non-fiction Writing at KS3* (1 85346 859 2). Published by David Fulton Publishers

SUMMER HOLIDAYS AT DOWNTOWN LEISURE CENTRE

Dear Young Member,

It's time again to write to you with news of all the activities we are providing for the holiday.

We have organised loads of activities, including:

- Multi Activity Days
- Bouncy Castle
- Swimming sessions
- Tennis and Squash
- Soft Play Sessions
- Keep Fit Classes
- Art and Craft Classes

Spaces are limited so BOOK NOW to avoid disappointment! You can book NOW for all these activities at the reception desk.

Yours in fun
Tim Smith, Leisure Centre Manager

Information Text 2

Text analysed: *Leisure centre leaflet*

Purpose • What is it for? • How do you know?	•
Audience • Who is it for? • How do you know?	•
Features at word level Think about: • specialised vocabulary • stock words and phrases	•
Features at sentence level Think about: • tense • length of sentences • structure of sentences • conjunctions and connectives • punctuation • 1st/2nd/3rd person • active/passive voice	•
Features at text level Think about: • layout • structure • sequence	•

Grid 3 Analysis of Information Text 2

Form: Information text – a letter to the parents of pupils in your year group giving details of a weekend trip to the theatre at the end of term

Purpose • What is it for?	• *To inform parents about trip* •
Audience • Who is it for?	•
Features at word level Think about: • specialised vocabulary • stock words and phrases	• *Form to send back at the end of letter*
Features at sentence level Think about: • tense • length of sentences • structure of sentences • conjunctions and connectives • punctuation • 1st/2nd/3rd person • active/passive voice	• *Future tense*
Features at text level Think about: • layout • structure • sequence	• *Subheadings to make sequence clear*

Grid 4 Writing an information text, with some examples to help in planning the text

Task 3: Analysing a high-quality information text

> ✍ **Notes for teachers**

- Look at the features of information texts that you have collected on grids so far.

  - *Consider audience and purpose.*
  - *Look at features at word, sentence and text level.*
  - *Look at examples of the nine purposes for writing identified in Task 2.*

- Mark examples of these features in Steve Jones's writing.

- Look at the purposes for writing listed on Grid 5. Identify which purposes Steve Jones has fulfilled and how he has done it. Fill in Grid 5.

  - *Model this process where necessary.*
  - *The fourth triplet – to analyse, review, comment – is introduced at this stage.*
  - *Pupils will probably discover that almost all the purposes can be identified. What seemed at first to be a 'scientific' text is in fact operating at many different levels on the reader.*

- What is the effect of the alternation between long and short sentences in this passage?

  - *This is an example of a question that can be asked to draw pupils' attention to the very deliberate nature of the writing. They may be much more accustomed to thinking about the author's intentions when considering fiction. This activity should impress upon them that non-fiction writers have designs on the reader too!*
  - *Possible answer: 'The long sentences are about the idealistic aims of the project; the short ones are about the brutal reality.'*
  - *Persuade pupils to move away from answers such as: 'It makes it more interesting; it makes you want to read on.'*
  - *Once they are talking about genuine effects, there is considerable room for profitable debate and difference of opinion. One reasoned explanation is as good as another.*

- What is the effect of the Biblical phrase 'sufficient unto itself'?

  - *It points up the folly of human beings who try to emulate God by creating their own world.*

- Write an answer to this question: How does Steve Jones make the writing of this information text vivid and interesting?

  - *This task reinforces the point that most texts are multi-purpose, that information has to be presented in an interesting way if it is to reach its audience.*
  - *There is an additional point to be grasped by the more sophisticated reader. This is in fact a biased text: it purports simply to be giving information while at the same time it systematically scorns the whole idea of the Biosphere.*
  - *Encourage pupils to choose specific words and phrases that add vividness to the text, to talk about them in detail, and then to frame some sentences that they can write down. You may wish to model this process yourself before asking pupils to attempt it.*

Task 3: Analysing a high-quality information text

- Look at the features of information texts that you have collected on grids so far.

- Mark examples of these features in Steve Jones's writing.

- Look at the purposes for writing listed on Grid 5. Identify which purposes Steve Jones has fulfilled and how he has done it. Fill in Grid 5.

- What is the effect of the alternation between long and short sentences in this passage?

- What is the effect of the Biblical phrase 'sufficient unto itself'?

- Write an answer to this question: How does Steve Jones make the writing of this information text vivid and interesting?

In the Arizona desert in the early 1990s an island was built. Biosphere Two, as it was called (the Earth itself was Biosphere One), tried to isolate itself from the pollution and vice around it. The plan was to create a world that never was – an unadulterated place in which man and Nature could live in harmony. Eight Biospherians set up a community sufficient unto itself, an ecosystem in the balance that had, they claimed, ruled our planet. The immense greenhouse was sealed off from the air as a two-hundred-million-dollar microcosm of diversity, from desert to rainforest to million-gallon ocean.

Within a year, its inhabitants faced reality. Microbes in the soil caused the amount of carbon dioxide to shoot up and the level of oxygen to fall to that on the summit of Mont Blanc. Vines strangled whole sections of the Biosphere as other plants died out. The animals had even less success. Nineteen of the twenty-five kinds of vertebrate perished, as did all the insect pollinators (which meant that most of the plants were doomed). The 'desert' grew grass and the water could be kept clean only by cutting great mats of algae. In 1994 the Biosphere was abandoned.

From *Almost Like A Whale*, by Steve Jones, Doubleday, 1999

Information Text 3

Text analysed:	
Purpose for writing	**How does Steve Jones fulfil it?**
1. to imagine	
2. to explore	
3. to entertain	
4. to inform	
5. to explain	
6. to describe	
7. to persuade	
8. to argue	
9. to advise	
10. to analyse	
11. to review	
12. to comment	

Grid 5 Analysis of Information Text 3

Investigating recount texts

✍ Notes for teachers

- A recount is a chronological retelling of events.

  - *What features would you expect in a text that is chronological, i.e. arranged according to the sequence of time?*
    - *that it tells some kind of story, with a beginning, middle and end;*
    - *that it is written in the past tense;*
    - *that it contains time connectives, such as 'then', 'later', 'after a while'.*

- Make a list with your partner of all the different kinds of recount text you know.

  - *Some newspaper stories, biography, autobiography, some school essays, some history writing, etc.*

- Collect as many recount texts as you can. What are the common features of recounts?

  - *Make this activity an investigation. Encourage pupils to look at as many texts as possible, looking for similarities but also for differences. Some recount texts give only facts; others mix fact with opinion; others show bias in a more subtle way; some, like Simon Schama below, are almost fictional recreations of a past event.*

- Read Recount Texts 1, 2 and 3.

  - *Allow pupils to enjoy the texts. Let them talk about their own childhood memories, or their own experiences of differing outlooks within families. Let them act out what Simon Schama is describing.*

- Use Grid 1 as the basis for your analysis of the texts.

  - *Model this process. It may be necessary to take the whole group through the process, working word by word and sentence by sentence through one of the texts, e.g. dealing with Text 2:*
    - *How is the passing of time conveyed in sentence 1?*
    - *What is the effect of the polysyllabic 'restlessness' in a sentence of monosyllables?*
    - *What is the effect of the everyday language of sentence 2, after the vagueness of the second part of sentence 1?*
    - *An example of how Grid 1 might be started for Text 2 is shown in Grid 2.*

- Report your analysis of one of the texts to the rest of the class or to a group within the class.

  - *Encourage pupils to make verbal reports of their findings, using their completed versions of Grid 1 as their notes for speaking.*
  - *If you want them to go on to write down their findings in continuous prose, encourage them to use the sentences that they spoke in their presentation as the basis for their writing. You may also need to model the writing.*

Task 1: Reading recount texts

- A recount is a chronological retelling of events.

- Make a list with your partner of all the different kinds of recount text you know.

- Collect as many recount texts as you can. What are the common features of recounts?

- Read Recount Texts 1, 2 and 3.

- Use Grid 1 as the basis for your analysis of the texts.

- Report your analysis of one of the texts to the rest of the class or to a group within the class.

© 2002 Paul Evans *How to Teach Non-fiction Writing at KS3* (1 85346 859 2). Published by David Fulton Publishers

My first word was bus. Apart from infantile renderings of 'Mummy' and 'Daddy' and 'Philip', bus was the first word I ever uttered. And throughout my childhood in Swansea I had a helpless passion for the great blood-red doubledeckers, and I would ride them, with no destination in mind, for hour after hour and day after day. Once, when I was seven or eight, I overheard a conversation between the bus-conductor – a much grander personage, then, with the metal ticket-dispenser strapped to his chest like a silver accordion – and one of his female passengers. She gave the name of her stop and said,

– I've been bad. Terrible I've been.

– Oh aye? It's the hospital then is it?

– Aye. Toothache.

– Have them all out and be done with it is what I say.

– Saves all the bother.

– Common sense.

Using the overhead strap, he leaned his face into hers, as if hesitating before a kiss, and out flashed the full vista of his flawless Chiclets.

– Ooh. Lovely. There's posh.

From *Experience*, by Martin Amis, Jonathan Cape, 2000

As the years passed, a restlessness began to grow upon her. She was unhappy, and at last she knew it. Mrs Nightingale, too, began to notice that there was something wrong. It was very odd; what could be the matter with dear Flo? Mr Nightingale suggested that a husband might be advisable; but the curious thing was that she took no interest in husbands. And with her attractions, and her accomplishments, too! ... Mrs Nightingale could not understand it; and then one day her perplexity was changed to consternation and alarm. Florence announced an extreme desire to go to Salisbury Hospital for several months as a nurse ...

A "nurse" meant then a coarse old woman, always ignorant, usually dirty, often brutal, a Mrs Gamp, in bunched-up sordid garment, tippling at the brandy bottle or indulging in worse irregularities ... It is not to be wondered at that her parents should have shuddered at the notion of their daughter devoting her life to such an occupation. "It was as if," she herself said afterwards, "I had wanted to be a kitchen-maid."

From 'Florence Nightingale', in *Eminent Victorians*, by Lytton Strachey, Chatto and Windus, 1918

At seven o'clock in the evening she returned to Marat's house, armed not just with the knife but with another letter imploring him to see her. Her arrival coincided with the delivery of fresh bread and the day's newspapers, so that she was already up the stairs when she was stopped by Simone herself [Marat's fiancée], who was suspicious of Charlotte's determination to see Marat. As they argued, Charlotte deliberately raised her voice to let Marat know that she wanted to give him special information about the traitors in Normandy. 'Let her in,' came the voice from the bath. She found him soaking, with the habitual wet cloth tied about his brow, an arm slung over the side of the tub. For fifteen minutes they talked about the situation at Caen, with Simone in attendance. Then Marat asked Simone to fetch some more kaolin solution for the water. To demonstrate her impeccable Jacobinism, Charlotte, in response to his request to name the plotters, recited a comprehensive list. 'Good,' replied Marat, 'in a few days I will have them all guillotined.'

Her chair was directly by the side of the bath. All she had to do was to rise, lean over the man, pull the knife out from the top of her dress, and lunge down hard and quickly.

From *Citizens*, by Simon Schama, Penguin, 1989

Text analysed:	
Techniques	**Effects**
At word level	
At sentence level	
At text level	

Grid 1 Analysing techniques and effects in recount texts

Text analysed: *Florence Nightingale*

Techniques	Effects
At word level 1. <u>Restlessness</u> is a vague word; <u>unhappy</u> is a bit clearer.	1. Takes the reader along with Florence's thought processes - as she gets clearer about what's wrong, so do we.
At sentence level 1. Sentences 3 and 5 are the thoughts of her parents but written as part of the text by the author.	1. The effect is to mock the parents because the sentences imitate gossipy speech.
At text level 1. Passage summed up by quote at the end.	1. Seems to prove that everything author has said about parents is true

Grid 2 An example of how Grid 1 might be started for analysing techniques and effects in recount texts

Task 2: Writing recount texts

✏ Notes for teachers

- Use the techniques that you identified in your analysis to write a few more sentences in the styles of Recount Texts 1, 2 and 3.

- *This activity forges the clear link between reading and writing. Pupils read as writers, picking out techniques and analysing their effect. Then they write as readers, deciding on the effects they wish to have on their readers and using the corresponding techniques.*

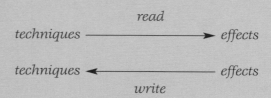

- Write about an everyday incident from your past in the style of Martin Amis.

- *Both this task and the next are a good preparation for Question 4 of Paper 1 in the Key Stage 3 English test. One of the choices invites pupils to write about an experience from their past. This is not, of course, a test of their memory, nor a genuine interest on the examiner's part in the lives of the candidates, but a test of how well they can write.*

- Write about a dramatic event from your past in the style of Simon Schama.

- *For this task and the previous one, encourage pupils to talk about events in their lives, to brainstorm ideas, to write down notes, words and phrases that are particularly effective, to tell others their ideas, and to embellish the truth to make a better story!*

- Write a recount for a newspaper article. Use Recount Text 4 as a model for your writing.

- *Go through the same process as above to identify the techniques and effects in the newspaper recount.*

Task 2: Writing recount texts

- Use the techniques that you identified in your analysis to write a few more sentences in the styles of Recount Texts 1, 2 and 3.

- Write about an everyday incident from your past in the style of Martin Amis.

- Write about a dramatic event from your past in the style of Simon Schama.

- Write a recount for a newspaper article. Use Recount Text 4 as a model for your writing.

$130,000 for a glob of ketchup

From PAUL THOMPSON in New York

A couple have been paid $130,000 compensation by Heinz after they discovered their ketchup bottle was underfilled by a TEA-SPOONFUL.

Bill and Marcia Baker spotted the tiny error when they poured the tomato sauce into a measuring cup while preparing a meatloaf recipe.

When they called in weights and measures officials they found the 20oz bottle was an ounce and a half short.

Heinz agreed to compensate Bill, 67, and Marcia, of Redding, California. But officials also found millions of other bottles were slightly short of sauce – so the firm agreed to overfill them by one per cent for a year.

It has cost Heinz an extra $600,000.

Michael Mullen, spokesman for Heinz, said: 'Once we realised there was a minute shortfall the company addressed the issue immediately.'

From *The Sun*, 28 May, 2001

Recount Text 4 A newspaper recount

Investigating explanation texts

Task 1: Reading explanation texts

✍ Notes for teachers

- Look at Explanation Text 1. This is an explanation of a relatively straightforward operation in Maths.

  - *Ask pupils to read the text and to explain it to each other. Then ask a pupil to demonstrate to the class or to a group the methods of addition that the text describes.*
  - *Ask pupils to comment on the effectiveness of the text in explaining what had to be done. The next three points draw attention to specific techniques that make the text effective. Pupils might identify others:*
    - *the straightforward structure of the sentences – no unnecessary diversions;*
    - *part of the plain, clear style is that there are no adjectives or adverbs;*
    - *the constant use of imperative verbs, giving a step-by-step series of orders.*

- How important is the layout in creating a text that is easily understood?

  - *The layout is unorthodox for a text – numbers used where one might expect words – lots of empty space on the page.*
  - *The layout creates clarity and a sense that, since there isn't much on the page, it must be relatively easy to work through.*
  - *Each major new element of the operation begins on the extreme left-hand side. The consecutive instructions in the middle of the text are lined up underneath each other half way across the page. This implicitly separates the new from the repetitive.*

- Note the patterns in the sentences: why are the sentences patterned in this way?

  - *Sentences begin with the purpose – to add . . . – and continue with the instruction.*
  - *When a series of instructions is required, each one is linked by the word 'then' – a technique that pupils will have been told many times not to use in their own writing!*
  - *But the use of the 'then' techniques illustrates fitness for purpose – the author is not after elegance here, but clarity.*

- Explain the use of italics.

  - *The italics serve to emphasise the main skill that is being developed in this exercise. There is no lengthy explanation of what working in your head means and why it is a good thing. The text encourages pupils to come to an understanding of those issues through practical, guided activity.*

Task 1: Reading explanation texts

- Look at Explanation Text 1. This is an explanation of a relatively straightforward operation in Maths.

- How important is the layout in creating a text that is easily understood?

- Note the patterns in the sentences: why are the sentences patterned in this way?

- Explain the use of italics.

© 2002 Paul Evans *How to Teach Non-fiction Writing at KS3* (1 85346 859 2). Published by David Fulton Publishers

Task 2: Writing explanation texts

✎ **Notes for teachers**

- Using Explanation Text 1 as a model, write an explanation of another mathematical operation, e.g. division or how percentages work.

- *This task will probably require a lot of oral preparation.*
- *Ask pupils to:*
  - *work out the explanation with a partner;*
  - *make notes that will help to sustain a verbal explanation;*
  - *try out their explanation on other pupils;*
  - *take feedback on the effectiveness of their explanation;*
  - *write the explanation and revise it in the light of feedback from others.*
- *You may wish to model the oral and written elements of this task.*

Task 2: Writing explanation texts

- Using Explanation Text 1 as a model, write an explanation of another mathematical operation, e.g. division or how percentages work. Use this page as a notepad. Write down ideas which will help you explain the operation to your partner.

© 2002 Paul Evans *How to Teach Non-fiction Writing at KS3* (1 85346 859 2). Published by David Fulton Publishers

To add a line of numbers, start at the left hand side:

Working in your head

6 + 4 + 3 + 8 = 21 add the first two numbers (10)
then add on the next number (13)
then add on the next number (21)

Check your answer by starting at the other end.

To add a column of numbers, start at the bottom and *working in your head* add up the column:

$$
\begin{array}{r}
8 \\
7 \\
2 \\
+\ 5 \\
\hline
22
\end{array}
\quad (5 + 2 = 7,\ 7 + 7 = 14,\ 14 + 8 = 22)
$$

Check your answer by starting at the top and add the column *in your head.*

From *STP National Curriculum Mathematics*, Stanley Thornes, 1995

Explanation Text 1 Explanation in Maths

Task 3: Reading explanation texts

✍ Notes for teachers

- Look at Explanation Text 2. This is a Key Stage 3 pupil's essay, explaining how the Plains Indians' way of life was damaged by the arrival of the Whites.

- *The pupil was given clear guidance on how to structure this essay. The following tasks encourage pupils to deconstruct the text, working out what that guidance entailed and how the pupil used it.*

- Consider the way in which it is organised. Work out why the writer has paragraphed the essay in this way. Pick out words and phrases that are used to give the text cohesion and to move it on to the next point.

- *The paragraphing matches the movement from one aspect of the question to the next, i.e.*
  - *opening statements that summarise the pupil's findings (para 1);*
  - *the use of reservations (2);*
  - *buffalo (3);*
  - *moving to another kind of bad influence (4);*
  - *school (5);*
  - *no ceremonies (6);*
  - *Christianity (7);*
  - *summary (8).*
- *Pupils could be encouraged to work out the kind of mapping that might have preceded the writing of this essay, e.g.*
  How were the Indians damaged?
  1 reservations;
  2 destruction of buffalo;
  3 being forced to be like Whites.
     a school;
     b. no ceremonies;
     c. Christianity.
- *Ask pupils to find text markers, e.g.:*
  - *'the long-term effect';*
  - *'from my research';*
  - *'perhaps the most significant change';*
  - *'equally important';*
  - *'firstly . . . secondly . . . thirdly'.*
- *Ask them to comment on their effectiveness.*

- Consider ways in which it might be improved.

- *For instance, pupils may want to develop points that are left largely unexplained, such as why farming broke down the Indians' tribal loyalties. They may feel that single sentence paragraphs need to be filled out with more detail or explanation.*

- After this discussion, re-write a part of the essay, making any changes that you feel would improve it. Be prepared to explain your changes, orally and in writing.

- *You may need to have some information on this topic available in the classroom.*

Task 3: Reading explanation texts

- Look at Explanation Text 2. This is a Key Stage 3 pupil's essay, explaining how the Plains Indians' way of life was damaged by the arrival of the Whites.

- Consider the way in which it is organised. Work out why the writer has paragraphed the essay in this way. Pick out words and phrases that are used to give the text cohesion and to move it on to the next point.

- Consider ways in which it might be improved.

- After this discussion, re-write a part of the essay, making any changes that you feel would improve it. Be prepared to explain your changes, orally and in writing.

How was the Indians' way of life changed by the Whites?

When the Whites came to America the Indians' life changed completely. The long-term effect is that they stopped the Indians being Indians. From my research it would seem that almost all information about the Indians came from the Whites' point of view. One wonders why this is.

Perhaps the most significant change in the lifestyles of the Indians happened when they were forced into reservations. These were small areas of land which the Indians were not allowed to leave. Moreover this meant that they could not move freely on their land but were confined in their reservations.

Equally important was the fact that the Whites killed all the buffalo. This was because they wanted the Indians to stay in their reservations so they killed all the buffalo so that the Indians would have no reason to leave the reservations. This meant that the Indians' main food source, the buffalo, had been taken away so naturally they began to farm. Farming broke down their tribal loyalties.

In addition to the two main factors above, the Whites did many things to make the Indians more like them.

Firstly, their children were made to go to school every day when before they never did.

Secondly, they were made to give up their dancing and ceremonies and to dispose of their own tribal costumes and wear Whites' clothing. They were not allowed to paint their faces and had to cut their hair short like the Whites.

Thirdly, they were made to go to church and become Christians, whereas before they had their own religions.

Overall, I think the Whites ruined the Indians' lifestyle by coming to America and because of what they did there are few true Indians left. I imagine that nowadays there are mixed feelings among the descendants of the Indians. Personally, I think that it's a great shame that their culture was ruined.

Explanation Text 2 Pupil's explanation writing in History

Task 4: Writing an explanation text

✍ Notes for teachers

- Write an essay entitled: 'How Advertisers Persuade Us To Buy Their Products'.

- Use the ideas in Explanation Text 3, and any others you can think of.
  - *Brainstorm other ideas, together with specific examples that pupils could link with each point.*

- Put each idea on a separate piece of paper, then put them in an order that you can justify.
  - *The physical manipulation of pieces of paper representing different ideas will help pupils to clarify and order their thoughts. Allow plenty of time for this, and for the articulation of their reasons for making their decisions.*
  - *Orders could include:*
    - *from most to least important;*
    - *from least to most important;*
    - *according to the different media in which advertisers work;*
    - *successful and unsuccessful attempts to persuade.*

- Work out how you are going to paragraph the essay.
  - *Each statement, each piece of paper, could represent the opening statement of a paragraph.*
  - *Each statement could be followed by examples to illustrate and justify the opening statement.*

- Work out the connective words and phrases that you will use to link one paragraph to the next.
  - *Pupils might use words and phrases that indicate addition, e.g. 'in addition', 'furthermore', 'secondly', etc.*
  - *They might use words and phrases that suggest a hierarchy, e.g. 'more importantly', 'but above all', 'the most widespread strategy', etc.*
  - *They might want to compare or contrast strategies by using words and phrases like 'similarly', 'again', 'likewise', 'in contrast', 'however', 'on the other hand', etc.*
  - *You can draw up lists of helpful connectives by modelling the writing yourself and by gathering examples from pupils.*
  - *You can encourage pupils to work in pairs on the opening sentences of paragraphs, and then discuss their effectiveness. See the description of supported composition in the Introduction pp. 5–10.*

- When you have checked over your essay, pass it to your partner for comment.
  - *Ensure that pupils review their own work thoroughly before passing it on to someone else.*
  - *Work out as a class a series of procedures through which a response partner has to go. Examples might include:*
    - *Is the organisation and structure of the work clear?*
    - *Does the paragraphing help to make the structure clear?*
    - *Are the links between the paragraphs clear?*
    - *Is the meaning of each sentence clear?*
    - *Are statements backed up by examples?*
    - *Is the use of vocabulary varied?*

- Write the final draft of your essay.

- Write a commentary on your essay, which explains how you constructed it.

- Writing a commentary on their own work achieves at least three important purposes for your pupils:
  - it makes them more conscious of the effects they are trying to achieve as writers;
  - it makes them think of themselves as writers, whose work is just as worthy of analysis as that of published authors;
  - it helps them to analyse the work of those published authors, having analysed themselves – you are much more likely to recognise how a published author constructs an argument when you have consciously tried to construct one yourself!
- You may need to model this part of the process, introducing phrases like:
  - 'I decided to put my ideas in order of...';
  - 'I wanted the best idea to come last because...';
  - 'In the third paragraph, I put the example before the statement to stop the whole thing becoming too predictable.'

Task 4: Writing an explanation text

- Write an essay entitled: 'How Advertisers Persuade Us To Buy Their Products'.

- Use the ideas in Explanation Text 3, and any others you can think of.

- Put each idea on a separate piece of paper, then put them in an order that you can justify.

- Work out how you are going to paragraph the essay.

- Work out the connective words and phrases that you will use to link one paragraph to the next.

- When you have checked over your essay, pass it to your partner for comment.

- Write the final draft of your essay.

- Write a commentary on your essay, which explains how you constructed it.

Advertisers use celebrities in their adverts.

Advertisers use humour in their adverts.

Adverts suggest that, to be cool, you have to have what they are advertising.

Advertisers appeal to greed.

Advertisers use sex in their adverts.

Advertisers use exotic locations.

Advertisers try to cash in on youth culture.

Advertisers suggest that their brand is better than that of their rivals.

Advertisers use mystery in their adverts, to intrigue customers.

Advertisers mock their own brands, to appear cool.

Advertisers sponsor popular events.

Advertisers use children's television, so that children will pester their parents to buy.

Advertisers use popular music.

Advertisers suggest that their brand is cheaper than that of their rivals.

Explanation Text 3 Ideas for essay paragraphs

Investigating instruction texts

Task 1: What is an instruction text?

✎ Notes for teachers

- Prepare to explain to your partner the rules of a simple game.

  - *You could make this a guessing game, if pupils conceal the name of the game from their partners.*
  - *The game will need to be simple rather than popular. The rules of football, for example, are probably too complex for this activity.*

- Make any written notes that you think may be appropriate.

  - *You may need to model this activity, to demonstrate the nature of notes to which one can speak. If they are too detailed, pupils will be tempted to read them out. The notes should be signposts, indicating to the speaker what the next point is. For example:*
    - *choose 'it';*
    - *run;*
    - *catch etc.*

- Explain the rules to your partner in one minute, and listen to her/his explanation.

  - *You may want to ask some pupils to give their talk to the whole class, so that you can model the evaluation process.*

- How effective were the instructions? How useful were the notes?

  - *What does 'effective' mean in this context?*
    - *If you play the guessing game, the ease with which it is possible to guess can be a gauge of effectiveness.*
    - *Can the person who hears the instructions then repeat them to a third party?*
    - *Were the instructions clear/interesting/concise?*
  - *Involve the pupils in drawing up the criteria of effectiveness.*
  - *In the same way, ask pupils to consider what makes notes useful. Pupils who bury their heads in pieces of paper rather than establishing eye contact are not using notes effectively.*

Task 1: What is an instruction text?

- Prepare to explain to your partner the rules of a simple game.

- Make any written notes that you think may be appropriate.

- Explain the rules to your partner in one minute, and listen to her/his explanation.

- How effective were the instructions? How useful were the notes?

© 2002 Paul Evans *How to Teach Non-fiction Writing at KS3* (1 85346 859 2). Published by David Fulton Publishers

Task 2: Reading instruction texts

✍ Notes for teachers

- Look at Instruction Text 1. On the box, the instructions appear under four drawings. What do you think the drawings depict? Are the instructions clear without the drawings?

- *Encourage pupils to sketch the drawings.*
- *The instructions are not at all clear unless the context is clear. If you did not know the instructions referred to Connect 4 – or did not know what Connect 4 is – they would be nonsensical.*

- Do a close analysis of the text at word, sentence and text level.

- *For example:*
  Word level
  - *technical vocabulary – 'tray'/'grid';*
  - *formal vocabulary – 'locate'/'reverse procedure'.*

  Sentence level
  - *imperative verbs – 'slide'/'reverse';*
  - *condensed language at start of sentences – 'to open'/'to close';*
  - *patterned language – 'to open'/'to close';*
  - *brackets – because it's obvious?*

  Text level
  - *drawings in original – make instructions clearer;*
  - *brief amount of text – to hold attention?*
  - *numbered points – emphasise sequence.*

Task 2: Reading instruction texts

- Look at Instruction Text 1. On the box, the instructions appear under four drawings. What do you think the drawings depict? Are the instructions clear without the drawings?

- Do a close analysis of the text at word, sentence and text level.

© 2002 Paul Evans *How to Teach Non-fiction Writing at KS3* (1 85346 859 2). Published by David Fulton Publishers

Connect 4
The original vertical strategy game

INSTRUCTIONS

1. To open – slide grid in either direction and locate in vertical position. (To close – reverse procedure and store in tray under grid.)

2. Each player takes 21 counters of one colour. Take turns to drop a counter into any of the slots in the grid.

3. The first player to get four in a row, either vertically, horizontally or diagonally wins the game.

4. At the end of the game simply raise the grid and tilt to release the counters.

From Connect 4 box, MB Games

Instruction Text 1

Task 3: Reading the hidden meanings in some instruction texts

✎ Notes for teachers

- One of the most common kinds of instruction text in schools is found in textbooks and on exam papers. These instructions are in code. Each subject has its own code.

  - *An essential part of tackling any question, whether from a textbook or from an exam paper, is talking through what is actually being required.*
  - *Encourage pupils to ask themselves the question: what will a successful answer look like?*
  - *A detailed look at exam criteria will be essential.*

- Look at Instruction Text 2. These questions demonstrate the code in English. You need to look for the imperative verbs, e.g. compare, explain and learn what they mean specifically in English.

  - *First of all, pupils need to ask themselves: what are we being asked to compare? In the case of question 1, it is the language of feelings/emotions/reactions.*
  - *Pupils need to find examples of such language, describe the technique being used and the effect of that technique, e.g.*

    Passage 1
    Technique   **Effect**

    Passage 2
    Technique   **Effect**

  - *Then they need to decide which techniques are similar and which are different, perhaps by putting ticks next to similarities and crosses next to differences.*
  - *They need the framework language for talking and writing about similarities and differences, e.g. 'likewise', 'similarly', 'in contrast', 'however'.*
  - *Finally, they need to know how much time to devote to the question and how much to write. In the particular case of the Key Stage 3 test, not much writing is required. Pupils must be trained to concentrate on a few, strong points, succinctly put.*

- Look also at the modal verbs, e.g. 'could', 'should'. Are these suggestions or orders?

  - *The modal verbs indicate that a list is coming which pupils can regard as a series of instructions. Pupils should be encouraged to use the lists as frameworks for their answers, until they become confident enough to create their own agendas for writing.*

- Look at textbooks and exam questions in other subjects. Pupils often find the language of questions a barrier. For instance, you might know how to do the Maths behind a question, but not actually show your ability because you do not understand the question. Learn to play the exam game – crack the code in each subject.

  - *This is clearly a big issue. It needs to be tackled throughout Key Stage 3 and across the whole curriculum, rather than solely in the run-up to SATs in Year 9 in only English, Maths and Science.*

Task 3: Reading the hidden meanings in some instruction texts

- One of the most common kinds of instruction text in schools is found in textbooks and on exam papers. These instructions are in code. Each subject has its own code.

- Look at Instruction Text 2. These questions demonstrate the code in English. You need to look for the imperative verbs, e.g. 'compare', 'explain', and 'learn' what they mean specifically in English.

- Look also at the modal verbs, e.g. 'could', 'should'. Are these suggestions or orders?

- Look at textbooks and exam questions in other subjects. Pupils often find the language of questions a barrier. For instance, you might know how to do the Maths behind a question, but not actually show your ability because you do not understand the question. Learn to play the exam game – crack the code in each subject.

Compare the two passages, commenting on the language the writers use to convey their reactions.

Explain how the writer has tried to make the description interesting.

Explain how the writer builds up suspense throughout this passage.

'Some people waste a lot of time and energy attempting difficult challenges, such as flying around the world in a hot-air balloon. Attempts like these are pointless, and benefit nobody.'

Write an article for your local newspaper, arguing <u>either</u> for <u>or</u> against statement.

In your article you could:
- explain which challenges you think are most worthwhile or pointless, and why;
- say why you think people take part in challenges;
- say which challenges, if any, you are interested in, and why;
- end by summing up your views for or against the statement.

How does Shakespeare make this scene interesting and tense for the audience?

Before you begin to write you should think about:
- the mood at the beginning of the scene and how this is interesting to the audience;
- how the characters' reactions to each other cause tension;
- how the language of the characters creates interest;
- what hints the audience gets about the future.

Adapted from English Key Stage 3 SATs papers, 2000

Instruction Text 2 Exam instructions

Task 4: Writing instruction texts

✍ Notes for teachers

- Use Instruction Text 1 and your analysis of it to write a set of instructions: directions to a place; rules for playing a game; recipes; instructions for assembly of a model or a piece of furniture; fitness/good health manuals, etc.

- Think about layout, format, illustrations.

- Write an analysis of your work at word, sentence and text levels when you have finished it.

- *Collect 'real life' examples of the texts that you want your pupils to create. Test the instructions, wherever possible, to see if they work, e.g. make the food that a recipe describes, build that bookcase. Enjoy yourselves, and establish that essential connection with the real world that instruction texts demand.*

- *There are many possibilities here for cross-curricular collaboration – ICT, design technology, art and design.*

- *The analysis helps to bring home to pupils that they are real writers, just like all the other authors whose work they analyse.*
- *The main criterion for evaluating the text is effectiveness, which will be linked to clarity, precision of language and conciseness. The texts should also be tested out, as suggested above.*

DIY FLATPACK FURNITURE

Task 4: Writing instruction texts

- Use Instruction Text 1 and your analysis of it to write a set of instructions: directions to a place; rules for playing a game; recipes; instructions for assembly of a model or a piece of furniture; fitness/good health manuals, etc.

- Think about layout, format, illustrations.

- Write an analysis of your work at word, sentence and text levels when you have finished it.

© 2002 Paul Evans *How to Teach Non-fiction Writing at KS3* (1 85346 859 2). Published by David Fulton Publishers

Task 5: An instruction too far

- Look at Instruction Text 3. Invent your own set of mindless instructions. Make a collection of any genuine examples you find.

- *Pupils might like to investigate the reasons for the appearance of such instructions. Perhaps they could contact manufacturers to find out why they do it.*

Task 5: An instruction too far

- Look at Instruction Text 3. Invent your own set of mindless instructions. Make a collection of any genuine examples you find. Use this page as a notepad.

© 2002 Paul Evans *How to Teach Non-fiction Writing at KS3* (1 85346 859 2). Published by David Fulton Publishers

On hairdryer: Do not use while sleeping

On bag of crisps: You could be a winner! No purchase necessary. Details inside.

On soap: Directions – Use like regular soap

On frozen dinner: Serving suggestion – Defrost

On shower cap: Fits one head

On dessert: Do not turn upside down (Printed on bottom of box)

On bread pudding: Product will be hot after heating

On iron: Do not iron clothes on body

On children's cough medicine: Do not drive car or operate machinery

On sleeping pills: Warning – may cause drowsiness

On Christmas lights: For indoor or outdoor use only

On peanuts: Warning – contains nuts

On packet of peanuts: Instructions – open packet, eat nuts

On chainsaw: Do not attempt to stop chain with hands

Instruction Text 3 Examples of genuine instruction texts

Investigating persuasion texts

Task 1: Writing persuasion texts

> ### ✍ Notes for teachers

- Imagine that you have created a new Internet service, which you want to persuade your friends to use.

  - *Go through the whole sequence of activities at the start, so that pupils know where the lesson is leading.*
  - *Pupils will need to look at some adverts for Internet services, and try to identify a gap in the market.*

- Devise a 30-second radio advert that will achieve your aim.

  - *Pupils should listen to some radio adverts and spend a short time analysing the techniques they use, e.g. dramatic scenarios with actors in role, 'in your face' shouting, music, humour, etc.*

- Try out your ideas orally.

  - *Pupils should work in pairs or small groups, revising ideas in the light of feedback.*
  - *Remember that the point of the exercise is to persuade young people to log on to the website.*

- Write your script and deliver it.

  - *You may want to encourage some pupils to deliver their script to the whole class, so that you can model the way in which you want the pupils themselves to comment on the techniques that they have used, and how you want other pupils to respond.*

- On your script, mark all the persuasive techniques that you have used.

  - *For example: arresting opening; imperative verbs; repetition; humour; the inclusion of young actors; a run through of what the website can do for the audience; a 'before-and-after' scenario.*
  - *Some techniques will not actually be apparent in a written script, e.g. accent, tone of voice, volume.*

- Ask your partner to comment on the effectiveness of your persuasion techniques.

  - *What was particularly effective? Why? What was not effective? Why not? What more do you need to know as a listener? What did you not need to know? Is it clear what you need to do next to access the website? Is the cost clear? Should it be?*

Task 1: Writing persuasion texts

- Imagine that you have created a new Internet service, which you want to persuade your friends to use.

- Devise a 30-second radio advert that will achieve your aim.

- Try out your ideas orally.

- Write your script and deliver it.

- On your script, mark all the persuasive techniques that you have used.

- Ask your partner to comment on the effectiveness of your persuasion techniques.

© 2002 Paul Evans *How to Teach Non-fiction Writing at KS3* (1 85346 859 2). Published by David Fulton Publishers

Task 2: Reading persuasion texts

✍ Notes for teachers

- Look at Persuasion Text 1.

- *Read the text aloud several times. Allow pupils to comment on any features they notice. Draw them into the crucial discussion about effect.*

- Analyse the text, using Grid 1 to help you.

- *The fact that the text is short allows pupils to do a full-scale analysis, which encourages them to demonstrate all the knowledge and understanding that they have acquired so far. If necessary, the suggestions shown in Grid 2 may be used.*

Task 2: Reading persuasion texts

- Look at Persuasion Text 1.

- Analyse the text, using Grid 1 to help you.

© 2002 Paul Evans *How to Teach Non-fiction Writing at KS3* (1 85346 859 2). Published by David Fulton Publishers

The **Guardian**

Get ahead not a headache

With Jobs Unlimited you can search all the Guardian's jobs online quickly and painlessly – and that's more jobs than any other national quality newspaper. The site does the work for you – just set up your personal search page and put your feet up while Jobs Unlimited finds, and saves, all suitable jobs. It'll help prevent looking for work becoming a real pain in the neck.

JobsUnlimited
www.jobsunlimited.co.uk

From the *Guardian Weekend Magazine*, 13 February 1999

Persuasion Text 1 Newspaper advert

Text analysed: *JobsUnlimited advert*

	Feature	Effect
Word level • Vocabulary	*Ahead/headache*	*Play on words/sets the theme of the advert/jokey.*
• Imagery		
• Recurrent words		
• Opinion/bias		
Sentence level • Punctuation	*No comma or full stop in headline*	*No comma brings head & headache closer/full stops not cool in headlines.*
• Nouns		
Text level • Audience	*Unemployed*	*It used to be bad to have no job - not any longer.*
• Purpose		
• Structure		

Grid 1 An analysis of Persuasion Text 1, with some suggestions to help you start

Text analysed: *JobsUnlimited advert*

	Feature	**Effect**
Word level		
• Vocabulary	*Quickly/painlessly/pain in the neck*	*Emphasise theme: this will take all your worries away.*
• Imagery	*Put your feet up*	*Finding a job is stressful – unless you do it this way.*
• Recurrent words	*Unlimited*	*There is definitely a job out there for you.*
• Opinion/bias	*More than any other national quality newspaper*	*Lots of them are rubbish – we're the best of the rest.*
Sentence level		
• Punctuation	*Dashes*	*Makes it sound more chummy – 2 different purposes: first an additional thought; second a new sentence.*
	Commas in 'finds, and saves,…'	*Emphasises how clever the program is.*
	`It'll	*Chummy again.*
• Nouns	*jobs/Guardian/jobs/jobs/ newspaper/site/work/page/ feet/jobs/jobs/work/pain/ neck*	*They tell the story of the advert/carry the main message.*
Text level		
• Audience	*Young people*	*This is a fast, modern solution to a temporary problem.*
• Purpose	*To get people to pay to log on to Guardian website*	*Why is cost not mentioned?*
• Structure	*Sentence 1 - the promise; 2 - how; 3 - joke .*	*It will be successful (1), easy (2), fun (3).*

Grid 2 An analysis of Persuasion Text 1: more suggestions

Task 3: Reading persuasion texts

✍ Notes for teachers

- Look at Persuasion Text 2.

- *The text is long, and may require you to use several different reading strategies, for example:*
  - *reading aloud, by you and/or pupils;*
  - *giving groups of pupils different paragraphs to read and summarise for the rest of the class;*
  - *cutting the article up into sections and asking pupils to put it back together in an order that makes best sense;*
  - *asking pairs to look at sections of the text, then asking one pupil to play the part of Matthew Parris, the other to play the part of an opponent of his ideas, so you get summary and counter-argument;*
  - *asking pupils to summarise the whole argument in 50 words/two sentences/one sentence.*

- The author, Matthew Parris, is saying that meat eating will die out, simply because people will come to realise that it is not a nice thing to do. The article is not polemical or preachy, but rather quietly persuasive.

- *The rest of this activity asks pupils to identify the tone of the writing and to analyse how that tone is achieved. This is subtle stuff. You may want to dramatise the issue to make it clearer, e.g.*
  - *ask a pupil to act the role of Mr/Mrs/Ms Nasty arguing a case – say, against corporal punishment : 'It's barbaric, degrading – only an animal would want . . . etc.'*
  - *now ask another pupil to be Mr/Mrs/Ms Nice arguing the same case – 'It's so much effort to swing that cane, and all to so little effect . . .'*

- Go through the article and underline the words and phrases that Parris uses to persuade the reader that eating meat is not nice.

- *Model this process.*
- *If the whole text is too daunting for some pupils, restrict them to a section of it. Tell them that in an exam, for instance, you would be expected only to identify a few examples.*

- Write each word and phrase on a separate piece of paper. See if you can put the pieces of paper into categories, so that you can generalise about the persuasive techniques that the author uses.

- *For example, you could list:*
  - *jokey title to get reader on author's side;*
  - *sentence structures to suggest that we are all rational people who share the same views, e.g. 'There can hardly be a thinking person...';*
  - *presentation of author's personality, as polite, British, hesitant, e.g. 'I hate to be a nuisance';*
  - *individual words which, beneath the genteel prose, show the horror of animal slaughter, e.g. 'slaughterhouses';*
  - *the author's genteel mockery of euphemism, e.g. 'culled';*
  - *phrase-making, e.g. 'bound for the butchers';*
  - *repetition, e.g. 'I...I...I'*

- Write an answer to the question: How does Matthew Parris try to convince his reader not to eat meat?

- *Encourage pupils to make notes from their discussions above.*
- *Model the process of turning notes in to a brief but coherent piece of continuous prose.*
- *There are two elements to the question. What are his arguments? How does he present them?*

Task 3: Reading persuasion texts

- Look at Persuasion Text 2.

- The author, Matthew Parris, is saying that meat eating will die out, simply because people will come to realise that it is not a nice thing to do. The article is not polemical or preachy, but rather quietly persuasive.

- Go through the article and underline the words and phrases that Parris uses to persuade the reader that eating meat is not nice.

- Write each word and phrase on a separate piece of paper. See if you can put the pieces of paper into categories, so that you can generalise about the persuasive techniques that the author uses.

- Write an answer to the question: How does Matthew Parris try to convince his reader not to eat meat?

Eating our fellow-mammals may not be wrong, but it is not very nice

MATTHEW PARRIS

There can hardly be a thinking person in Britain who has not, over the last few weeks, thought again about eating meat. For me the pause for reflection began when, after penning for the *Times* a rather gushing lament for the ascending souls of the hundreds of thousands of 'culled' animals which were dying all at once, I heard on the news that this total, though huge, was dwarfed by the numbers of animals who die every week as a matter of course in slaughterhouses, bound for the butchers.

The intention of the politicians in disclosing these figures was to persuade us that the cull wasn't quite as ghastly as the raw numbers might suggest. The effect on me was the opposite: I wondered again, and more urgently, whether it is acceptable, for us who do not need to, to eat meat.

And then all the arguments the other way, the arguments I know so well and have repeated to myself so often, came trotting back. I wear leather shoes and belts. I buy a bewildering variety of products whose ingredients include animal matter. I travel to places where a vegetarian would starve. I hate to be a nuisance. I couldn't bear to sound self-righteous at dinner parties. Fish may also feel some pain.

And, most of all, I love meat.

All these arguments, none of them trivial, I considered again. But then a new thought struck me. I have never believed that life is sacred, only good. I have never believed that the infliction of suffering is wholly avoidable, only to be avoided where conveniently possible. I have never believed that we must not kill, only that we should restrict our murders to the minimum.

I am no Brahmin. Why then was I entertaining the argument about vegetarianism as though it were a clash of absolutes: as though, if one believed it was a pity to kill other animals, one must so organise one's life that in no circumstances and however peripherally was one involved in their death?

From whom, after all, do we most commonly hear vegetarianism examined as though it were a claimed absolute? From scornful meat-eaters who wish to ridicule vegetarians. And why do those carnivores urge what they say are the logical conclusions to a vegetarian's claims? To push him into stricter vegetarianism? No. They want to insinuate that if you can't go all the way, then it isn't even worth setting out.

And all at once it was obvious. There is no need to stop eating meat to start becoming a vegetarian. The beginning of wisdom on this question is the recognition that 'vegetarian' is a word like 'disciplinarian' or 'agrarian': you can be more or less of one. It is not a word like 'octogenarian' – where you are or you aren't.

The way forward for me was suddenly clear. I shall eat less meat. When it is served to me by hosts I shall gratefully accept, because I like meat and don't want to spoil the party. But I shall stop buying meat myself, and in restaurants where there is an alternative I'll order the alternative. And if many others begin to do the same, then more restaurants will offer more alternatives, and more supermarkets will stock less meat and more vegetarian food. The market for meat will shrink, the economies of scale disappear and the shift will gather pace.

It is under way now. A tide of moral sentiment is slowly turning. It turns first in the unconscious mind. We feel not *opposed* to something, but vaguely uncomfortable about it.

When a practice, such as killing animals for our table, is moving into the realms of those things we will no longer contemplate anyone doing, a reliable early warning is when we start preferring not to do it ourselves. For most folk that point was passed centuries ago. The next landmark comes when not only would we rather not do it ourselves, but we would rather not even see it done. Today, I doubt whether one in 100 of our citizens could with equanimity spend a morning in a slaughterhouse (note, for it is notable, the arrival of a French euphemism for 'slaughterhouse').

Finally comes the landmark which signals an imminent shift in behaviour. We would rather not even think about it being done. Were I to dwell, here, on the details of how animals are slaughtered for the table, you – for whose table they are slaughtered – would rightly fault me for lack of taste.

I could press this argument, but do not need to. Eating our fellow-mammals, now that we no longer need to, isn't especially nice, and in our hearts we know it, every one of us. This truth, far from being undermined by the anger carnivores feel towards vegetarians, explains the anger.

Further argument is unnecessary, not least because I am not proposing that anyone should be forbidden to eat meat.

This thing is going to happen without anybody being deprived of anything they strongly desire. You and I can help make it happen without any serious disruption to our lives. We need make no sweeping resolutions at all. We can be part of an incremental switch.

Painless programmes for self-improvement should normally be treated with suspicion. Suggestions that we could lose weight without ever feeling hungry, give up heroin without going cold turkey, chuck smoking without withdrawal symptoms, or become teetotallers yet never crave a drink, rarely amount to more than hype. To stress, to a person anxious to quit a pleasurable but unwelcome habit, that iron discipline will be required and the experience may hurt, is a useful thing to do because that is no less than the truth, and helps the individual prepare himself mentally for the struggle.

But the ending of modern man's dependence on meat will be different. There will be no countrywide campaigns of total abstention. There will be no bans, no health warnings, no punitive excise duties. There will be no moral imperative never to touch another slice of bacon, no pariah-carnivores, no meat-junkies guiltily chewing pepperoni sausage in office doorways. Giving up meat does not call for any stampede into soya – any massed, shuddering, national retreat from an unacceptable habit.

It will be a very gradual change of taste, driven not by dogma nor by any absolute objection to eating animals, but by the urge of which any higher order is conscious: to civilise itself. It will not be complete in any of our lifetimes.

But it is well under way already. The argument can cease.

From the *Spectator*, 21 April 2001

Persuasion Text 2 Magazine article *continued*

Task 4: Reading persuasion texts

✍ Notes for teachers

- Look at Persuasion Text 3.

- *Use the strategies suggested above to encourage pupils of all abilities to engage with longer texts. This must be an empowering rather than a dispiriting process. You do not have to master every word of the text in order to complete the task successfully.*

- Summarise Philip Hensher's argument against the Harry Potter books in 100 words.

  The main points seem to be:
  - *The books have no literary merit, because:*
    - *too readable;*
    - *endless series of events – and then . . . and then . . . ;*
    - *conventional boarding school;*
    - *not as good as LeGuin.*
  - *Mistake to make Dursleys evil.*
  - *Can only be read once as intended, i.e. 11-year-olds growing up to 17-year-olds.*
  - *Adults are pretending to like them.*

- Read your summary to your partner. Check each other's work, to make sure that it is clear and includes all the main points.

  - *Encourage pupils to maintain Hensher's tone in this exercise.*

Task 4: Reading persuasion texts

- Look at Persuasion Text 3.

- Summarise Philip Hensher's argument against the Harry Potter books in 100 words.

- Read your summary to your partner. Check each other's work, to make sure that it is clear and includes all the main points.

© 2002 Paul Evans *How to Teach Non-fiction Writing at KS3* (1 85346 859 2). Published by David Fulton Publishers

Task 5: Writing persuasion texts

✍ Notes for teachers

- As you did with Persuasion Text 2, categorise some of Hensher's persuasion techniques. He is much more aggressive in his arguments, but he also tries to 'knock out' the other side of the argument before getting to his own views, by rehearsing examples of the huge success of the Harry Potter books.

- Do you want to be a Parris or a Hensher? Use some of Parris's and/or Hensher's techniques in a piece of writing of your own. You should write either for or against an attitude, a behaviour, a viewpoint, a book, a film, a pop group, etc.

- *You can set up an opposition between the techniques of Parris and Hensher.*
- *Take any topic, e.g. smoking. How would Parris argue against it? 'It is gradually becoming regarded as terribly uncivilised to pollute the atmosphere. . . .' How about Hensher? ' They cough their guts up, and expect us to pay their hospital bills.'*

Pupils will need to:
- *choose a subject;*
- *marshall their arguments (which should all be either for or against a proposition);*
- *decide which of Parris's and/or Hensher's persuasion techniques they will use;*
- *try out sentences and paragraphs orally with a partner;*
- *reflect after writing on the effectiveness of their writing.*

Task 5: Writing persuasion texts

- As you did with Persuasion Text 2, categorise some of Hensher's persuasion techniques. He is much more aggressive in his arguments, but he also tries to 'knock out' the other side of the argument before getting to his own views, by rehearsing examples of the huge success of the Harry Potter books.

- Do you want to be a Parris or a Hensher? Use some of Parris's and/or Hensher's techniques in a piece of writing of your own. You should write either for or against an attitude, a behaviour, a viewpoint, a book, a film, a pop group, etc.

© 2002 Paul Evans *How to Teach Non-fiction Writing at KS3* (1 85346 859 2). Published by David Fulton Publishers

Harry Potter – Give me a Break

'When people quite seriously start to talk about these books as classics, to think of them in terms of the Whitbread Prize, it's time to worry'

By **Philip Hensher**

The on-line bookshop Amazon.com publishes an on-going bestseller list of the books most in demand by its readers at any given moment. It makes fascinating reading, listing as it does hundreds of thousands of books in order of their popularity. At present, number one on the list, narrowly beating Delia Smith and Frank McCourt, is one of JK Rowling's Harry Potter books. It is the fourth volume in the series.

Nothing surprising in that; as everyone knows, Harry Potter is enormously popular, and the books have proved a great success with all sorts of readers. There's only one thing about this that might cause the eyebrows to raise a little. The fourth volume of Harry Potter hasn't been published yet, and won't be until July. Amazon's bestseller, in short, is a book that doesn't exist.

The Harry Potter story has been told a thousand times by now, and the colossal success of the series shows no sign of abating. Indeed, if anything, enthusiasm seems to be growing as word-of-mouth spreads beyond the traditional book-reading classes. How JK Rowling, a single mother, mapped out a series of books about a schoolboy wizard after giving up on an unsatisfactory marriage to a Portuguese drop-out; how she wrote the first book in cafés to keep warm, since she could not afford to heat her flat.

The first volume was published, launched with little in the way of fanfare – and then it took off, making its way from hand to hand in the classroom. Children who had previously shown no interest in reading could suddenly be found in the corners of the playground with a copy of *Harry Potter and the Philosopher's Stone.*

Miraculously, children seemed willing to stretch themselves by deciphering unfamiliar words, just to be able to read about Harry Potter and his marvellous adventures. The second volume, *Harry Potter and the Chamber of Secrets*, was an even bigger success, and by the time of the third volume, Bloomsbury found it necessary to delay the publication time until the afternoon, so great was the risk that children would bunk off school to buy a copy of *Harry Potter and the*

Prisoner of Azkaban. For days afterwards, the high streets were filled with children reading as they walked, quite unable to put the thing down.

An amazing phenomenon. JK Rowling has encouraged children to read a book, to acquire the habit of reading, and has done it with books that stretch them with unfamiliar vocabulary. They read them, and then they read them again, over and over and over. But, even more extraordinarily, the phenomenon didn't stop there. Parents started reading the books themselves; Bloomsbury rather brilliantly noticed the number of fathers who were – slightly shamefacedly – reading the Harry Potter books on the Tube to work, and brought out adult editions in groovy black-and-white.

Everyone, it seems, loves Harry Potter. The third volume has been nominated for the Whitbread Children's Book Award, to be announced tonight. But plenty of voices have been raised to suggest that the Children's Book Award is not enough for these marvellous books; that nothing less than the overall Whitbread Prize will do. William Hill, which is running a book on the main prize, makes our bespectacled hero 2–1 joint favourite – tied with Seamus Heaney, no less.

At which point, it is time to say 'Enough'. No, really, enough of Harry Potter. It is all getting seriously out of hand, and, hugely beneficial as the books have been in encouraging young readers, it is time to say that there is a limit to what can be said about them. We shouldn't confuse the success of the pedagogic tool with literary merit. The books virtually read themselves, and that is admirable. If we ask, however, if they are really remarkable books, it is hard to think that they are. And if, as the Whitbread judges ought to, we go on to ask if the books hold the promise of becoming classics, of having real literary merit, then the answer is pretty definitely no.

They are written in a way which is designed to be seductively readable; they never give way to reflection or those momentary flashbacks of recall that prove so confusing to young readers, but exist in a sort of 'And then, and then, and then' which children find irresistible. But the world of these books is thin and unsatisfactory, their imagery is derivative, their characterisation automatic, and their structure deeply flawed. If I had read them when I was seven years old, I would have loved them, just as I loved *In The Fourth Form At Mallory Towers*. But I am not seven years old, and can see a little better than I could then whether a book's appeal stands some chance of lasting in a reader's affections. The Harry Potter books do their job, and it does them no favours at all to talk about them in terms of literary classics.

Children like them, in part, because they know all about the Billy Bunter conventions of the boarding-school story, and like to see the conventions gone through one more time. The world of prefects and detention, of masters in gowns, of school lacrosse matches, somehow filters down to children, and they are reassured by the closed, certain world. They know, too, exactly what they want to see when it comes to magic and the supernatural, and the books run through the conventions of spells, broomsticks, witches and wizards without a second thought. Nothing at all unfamiliar here. Children like, too, the romance structure, which carefully follows the analysis laid down by narratological theorists of the folk-tale; like all heroes of romance, Harry Potter is an orphan – his origins uncertain – who is in possession of great gifts.

Nothing unfamiliar at all, and if the general idea is taken from the most universal and unremarkable stock of children's book ideas, a lot of the detail is borrowed from specific classics. The recurrent idea of the jellybeans in which every imaginable flavour may be found is pure *Charlie and the Chocolate Factory*. Much of the detail of the school is taken from a marvellous classic, Ursula K LeGuin's *A Wizard of Earthsea*. Here may be found the duels between wizards, the laborious lessons in specific wizarding crafts, and, most strikingly, the supercilious aristocratic pupil who is an enemy of the hero. The Harry Potter books and LeGuin's Earthsea books are in different registers, that is all; one is set in a comic version of England, the other in an incantatory mythical world. One is a masterpiece, the other performs a useful function. To read the unforgettably terrifying second volume, *The Tombs of Atuan*, in LeGuin's series after the search for the

Basilisk in *Harry Potter and the Chamber of Secrets* is to see the difference between a visionary imagination and one that runs along pre-set grooves.

And a great deal of what Rowling adds to the mixture is not noticeably successful. It's a bad mistake to make Harry's non-magical uncle and aunt actually evil, and get their enjoyment out of starving Harry in the garret. I can see why she did it; it worked very well indeed for Roald Dahl in *James and the Giant Peach*. But with a real monster, Lord Voldemort, on the loose, it raises unhelpful questions about whether they are in league with the magical forces of evil, which will at some point have to be answered one way or another, and either answer is going to make their earlier behaviour seem less credible.

It's also a bad misconception to think of the audience for Harry Potter growing up with him, and introducing more and more serious issues with each annual title. It sounds like a good idea now, when the audience really is going to grow up with the hero, and the 11-year-olds who read the first Harry Potter are going to be 17 for the last volume, and sharing his agonies over girls and campaigning against global warming, or whatever. But once the books have all been published, no one is ever going to read them like that – one a year – again, and the series will seem badly lopsided to any child reader.

Of course, to children these books are a very good thing, and no one can doubt that a lot of Harry Potter's enthusiastic young readers are going to go on to read much better books; books, moreover, that they might never have reached without that initial encouragement.

What we ought to worry about is the infantilisation of adult culture, the loss of a sense of what a classic really is. Grown men and women go to the cinema to see Disney cartoons, and no one thinks it surprising. But when people quite seriously start to talk about these books as classics, to think of them in terms of the Whitbread Prize, it's time to worry.

To look at David Cairns's unforgettably honest and harrowing biography of Berlioz; to read Seamus Heaney's *Beowulf* volume and then, perfectly seriously, propose that *Harry Potter and the Prisoner of Azkaban* deserves a prize because Jack and Chloe just couldn't put it down? Please, do us a favour – grow up.

From *The Independent*, 25 January, 2000

Persuasion Text 3 Newspaper article *continued*

Investigating discursive texts

Task 1: Reading discursive texts

✍ Notes for teachers

- Look at Discursive Text 1. It is a history essay, written by a Key Stage 3 pupil.

- *The models for most of the texts that pupils are required to write at Key Stages 3 and 4 cannot be found in textbooks. History teachers do not want pupils to write in the style of history textbooks, and so on. The models for writing will come mainly from two sources; texts that teachers construct at the front of the classroom through modelled and shared writing; texts that pupils have written, which can be used as guides for other pupils, illustrating both strengths and weaknesses.*

- Find the evidence about Cromwell's life, around which the essay is built. Decide whether the writer has used each piece of evidence as an indication that Cromwell was a hero or a villain. Indicate the line number where each piece of evidence has been used. Use Grid 1 to help you.

- *This task involves deconstructing the way in which the pupil was taught how to write this essay: find evidence about Cromwell's activities; categorise them as the actions of a hero or villain; decide how the points should be linked together; make an appropriate choice of connective signpost.*

- Now look at how the writer has used connecting words and phrases to link the text together. Collect all the connecting words and phrases and categorise them on Grid 2.

- *Pupils should categorise all of the following: as (3); maybe (6); on the one hand (7); even if (8); it is clear (9); this shows that (11); he was said to have (13); on the other hand (16); is an example of this (18); shows that (19); even though (19); again (21); it seems that (21); this seemed (22); however (22); it may have been that (22); appears (25); for example (25); although (29); it is possible (30); moreover (34); may have been (36); true (39); but (39); to sum up (43); then (43); while (44); in my opinion (44); overall (45); what is certain (47).*

Task 1: Reading discursive texts

- Look at Discursive Text 1. It is a history essay, written by a Key Stage 3 pupil.

- Find the evidence about Cromwell's life, around which the essay is built. Decide whether the writer has used each piece of evidence as an indication that Cromwell was a hero or a villain. Indicate the line number where each piece of evidence has been used. Use Grid 1 to help you.

- Now look at how the writer has used connecting words and phrases to link the text together. Collect all the connecting words and phrases and categorise them on Grid 2.

© 2002 Paul Evans *How to Teach Non-fiction Writing at KS3* (1 85346 859 2). Published by David Fulton Publishers

Oliver Cromwell, Hero or Villain?

Oliver Cromwell. A man whose life is a complete mystery. There are many different views about him. He was honest, a brilliant general, not power mad but sometimes very brutal. Nobody really knows, as the people who wrote about him were either strongly in favour of him or

5 *strongly against him. In this essay I am going to try to sort out some of these opinions and maybe come to some sort of decision.*

On the one hand, Oliver Cromwell was a brilliant general who won the war against the odds. He made England strong and respected even if he did do this in a brutal way. It is clear from Oliver Cromwell's letter to

10 *the House of Commons in September of 1649 that he was able to achieve decisive victories. This shows that he organised his army well and they listened and responded in an organised fashion. He was said to have created the best army England had ever had (the New Model Army). He kept going and he did not give up, winning the respect of*

15 *many people.*

On the other hand, Cromwell's hard, cruel side sometimes seemed to shine out, a side that not many people had seen before he came to power. The massacre at Drogheda is an example of this. His letter to the House of Commons shows that, even though this was a brutal thing

20 *to do, he believed it was what he had to do.*

Again, it seems that Oliver Cromwell was behind the King's execution. This seemed a brutal thing. However, it may have been that when Cromwell tried to reason with the King he turned him down, then secretly gathered another army to start another war.

25 *Oliver Cromwell appears to have been an honest man. For example, when his portrait was painted he told the artist to paint him exactly as he saw him, wrinkles, pimples and warts. This honesty was also reflected in the way his army was run. He listened to the army about not becoming king, although if he did he wouldn't have the support of the army which*

30 *would make it almost impossible to run the country. It is possible that he just did not want to be king and saw the army's objections as the way out.*

Moreover, Cromwell was a man who believed in equal rights. He fought

35 *for what he believed in and he did everything for a reason. The supposedly meaningless attack on Drogheda may have been for a reason. The Catholics in his eyes used jewelry and power to represent God. This he did not believe in and thought it his right to do something about it. True, these actions may not have been the right ones in our eyes, but*

40 *Oliver Cromwell thought he was doing them for the good of the country and his religion.*

To sum up, then, is Oliver Cromwell a hero or a villain? Hard to say. While it is true that he did some terrible things, in my opinion they

45 *were all for an honest reason. Overall, he made England more organised and respected, which many Kings and Queens could not manage. What is certain is that Oliver Cromwell will remain a puzzle and a cause of argument for many people in years to come.*

Discursive Text 1

	Text analysed: *Oliver Cromwell essay*	
Line number	**Hero**	**Villain**
7	*brilliant general*	
21		*King's execution*

Grid 1 Analysis Discursive Text 1

Text analysed: *Oliver Cromwell essay*

Similarity	**Difference**
Also (line 27)	*On the other hand (16)*
Cause and effect	**Adding**
As (3)	*Again (21)*
Conceding	**Illustrating**
Even though (19)	*For example (25)*
Emphasising	**Summarising**
It is clear (9)	*To sum up (43)*
Other signposts	**Other signposts**

Grid 2 Connectives as signposts

Task 2: Writing discursive texts

✍ Notes for teachers

- Take as your subject a character in a novel or short story you have read recently. The title for your writing is: (Character's name): Hero(ine) or Villain(ness)?

- *Pupils are using the Cromwell essay as the model for this writing.*
- *The criteria by which their writing will be judged are:*
  - *is there a balance of argument and counter-argument?*
  - *is evidence supplied to justify each point?*
  - *is a full range of appropriate connectives used?*

- You have just deconstructed an essay: now you have to put all the pieces back together again. Use Grids 3 and 4 to plan your essay.

- Practise speaking sentences and paragraphs to your partner before writing them down.

- *The whole task could be undertaken orally before the essays are written. A series of pupils could speak arguments and counter-arguments in front of a group or the whole class.*
- *Prepare a list of appropriate connectives which can be displayed in the classroom at the time of the speaking and the writing.*
- *By rehearsing sentences before they are written, pupils continue to develop their 'feel for the sentence'. They also get into the habit of revising their work before they write it down. This is a valuable skill to acquire in preparation for exams, where there is usually not time or inclination to re-read and re-draft.*
- *Take some time to work on individual sentences. At a certain point, ask all pupils to work out in their heads the next sentence of a text. Then ask them to tell their partners the sentence. If their partners' sentences are in some way better, then pupils can change their own sentences to accommodate the improvement. Then ask pupils to go round the room and listen to lots of other sentences. The idea is to return to your seat with the best possible sentence. When pupils return to their places, ask them to speak their best sentence out loud. Only after they have rehearsed it a few times are they allowed to write it down.*
- *Make this technique – mental rehearsal – an explicit part of every pupil's strategy for improving writing.*

Task 2: Writing discursive texts

- Take as your subject a character in a novel or short story you have read recently. The title for your writing is: (Character's name): Hero(ine) or Villain(ness)?

- You have just deconstructed an essay: now you have to put all the pieces back together again. Use Grids 3 and 4 to plan your essay.

- Practise speaking sentences and paragraphs to your partner before writing them down.

....: Hero(ine) or Villain(ness)?

Hero(ine)	Villain(ness)
Evidence (including page number)	Evidence (including page number)

Grid 3 Planning discursive writing: arguments and counter-arguments

When I want to draw attention to a similarity, I will use these words and phrases:

When I want to draw attention to a difference, I will use:

When I want to link cause and effect, I will use:

To add a further point, I will use:

To concede a point, I will use:

To illustrate a point, I will use:

To emphasise a point, I will use;

To sum up, I will use:

There are other purposes for which I want to use connectives as signposts.
<u>Purpose</u>   <u>Connectives</u>

Grid 4 Planning discursive writing: connectives as signposts

Task 3: Writing discursive texts

✍ Notes for teachers

- You are going to write an essay on the following subject: 'Should popstars be role models for young people?'

- *A brainstorm or discussion that brings out many points could precede the ordering of ideas that Grid 5 prompts.*
- *Pupils could write each idea on a separate piece of paper and move the pieces around until they are satisfied with their categorisation.*

- Use Grid 5 to help you to devise your arguments for and against.

- *Help pupils to group their ideas into paragraphs that begin with topic sentences – sentences that state the big idea for that paragraph. This BIG POINT can then be followed by little points which explore, clarify, develop, amplify and exemplify the BIG POINT.*

- Use Grid 6 to draw up a list of connectives that you will use.

- *Pupils should be encouraged to add to the list in Grid 6, thereby proving to themselves that they are in control of the language of essay writing. They should also be encouraged to speak their sentences before they write them down, so that as much of the editing process as possible has been achieved before any actual writing has been done. Pupils will also get the 'feel' for this kind of writing much more easily if they can express their ideas clearly in speech.*

Task 3: Writing discursive texts

- You are going to write an essay on the following subject: 'Should popstars be role models for young people?'

- Use Grid 5 to help you to devise your arguments for and against.

- Use Grid 6 to draw up a list of connectives that you will use.

Title: *Should popstars be role models for young people?*

Arguments for	Arguments against
BIG POINT 1 • *They show what determination can achieve.* Little points to back up BIG POINT 1 • *Real-life example of someone who came from hard background.* • *Real-life example of someone who was inspired by a star to become one him/herself.*	BIG POINT 1 • *They waste their wealth.* Little points to back up BIG POINT 1 • *Real-life example of someone who wastes their money.* • *Real-life example of someone who decided to change and do something useful with his/her wealth.*
BIG POINT 2	BIG POINT 2
BIG POINT 3	BIG POINT 3
BIG POINT 4	BIG POINT 4

Grid 5 Planning discursive writing: arguments and counter-arguments for popstars essay

Connectives for popstars essay
To compare: Likewire Equally
To contrast: Whereas On the other hand
To illustrate: For example As shown by
To sequence: Secondly Finally
To qualify: However And yet
To add: Also Moreover
To link through cause and effect: Therefore Consequently
To give a personal response: In my opinion This tells me that
To give alternatives: It could be argued that It is possible that

Grid 6 Planning discursive writing: connectives for popstars essay

Task 4: Writing discursive texts

✍ Notes for teachers

- You are going to write an essay on a Shakespeare play, with particular emphasis on one scene, which you have studied thoroughly.

- *The writing should be the culmination of a whole series of activities, most of which should be oral. Notes relevant to the written task could be made at appropriate moments.*
- *Activities which have a direct bearing on the writing of this essay could include:*
  - *debating the moral issues underlying the play;*
  - *rehearsing pivotal scenes in modern language and settings;*
  - *forum theatre, in which some pupils assume the roles of the characters while the rest of the class act as the directors of the scene, giving directions on movement, gesture, tone, volume etc.;*
  - *debating central images or words in a scene and their significance for the scene and the play as a whole;*
  - *hotseating, in which pupils assume the roles of the characters and are questioned about their actions and feelings by the rest of the class;*
  - *debating similarities and differences between characters;*
  - *making statements about characters and scenes and then arguing a different interpretation.*
- *Pupils should be thoroughly familiar with every aspect of a scene before being required to write about it in the way described below.*

- Use Grids 7 to 12 to help you to construct the essay.

- *Pupils could be encouraged to invent a mnemonic to help them to remember the categories which they should include in their writing, i.e.*
  S(ummary)
  C(ontext)
  C(haracters)
  A(ctions)
  L(anguage)
  S(taging)
- *They should also be encouraged to talk through sections before they write, as they are planning, and just before they write the definitive version. Encourage them to invent their own helpful connectives.*
- *Model speaking and writing regularly, e.g. when writing about context:*
  'The mixture of fear and extreme violence that he exhibits in this scene for the first time characterises his behaviour throughout the rest of the play.'
- *Train them to list and memorise useful words to describe the characters, actions and language of the scene that you are studying, e.g.*
  - *Characters – indecisive/imaginative/ambitious*
  - *Actions – climax/anti-climax/cause/consequence*
  - *Language – excessive/hallucinatory/abrupt*

Task 4: Writing discursive texts

- You are going to write an essay on a Shakespeare play, with particular emphasis on one scene, which you have studied thoroughly.

- Use Grids 7 to 12 to help you to construct the essay.

Summary of the scene
• **Summarise the events of the scene, in a few sentences.**
• **Say why the scene is important in the play.**
• **Outline briefly the changes that take place in the scene, in terms of plot and character.**
• **Choose a few words from the scene that sum up what it is about, and explain your choice.**
Helpful connectives. • In brief/to sum up/briefly/in summary/in essence/essentially • The importance of the scene lies in the fact that/the reason why • The main change that takes place/I say this because • The following words sum up the scene:/this quote shows that/when Shakespeare uses the word.../using the word...shows that

Grid 7 Planning a Shakespeare essay: summarising the scene

The context of the scene

- **Look back in the play, and explain briefly how the characters came to be in the situation which we see in the scene.**

- **Look forward, and explain how the actions, decisions and attitudes that characters take in this scene influence what happens to them later in the play.**

Helpful connectives
- In earlier scenes/previously we have seen/this behaviour is first evident/this reminds the audience of
- This attitude appears again/this foreshadows/here begins the build-up that culminates/we see this again later

Grid 8 Planning a Shakespeare essay: the context of the scene

Characters

- **Write mainly about the characters mentioned in the question. Quote briefly what they say, and then explain how their words indicate their personalities, thoughts and feelings.**

- **Write about the changes that characters go through in the scene, and explain why and how they go through them.**

Helpful connectives
- When...says '...', this tells the audience that/...'s use of the word '...' indicates that/this may indicate that/... on the other hand, it could be argued that...
- This change happens gradually through the scene...first..., secondly,... finally/the reason for the change could be/this action precipitates the change from...to...

Grid 9 Planning a Shakespeare essay: the characters

Actions

- **Write a very brief summary of what the characters do.**

- **Explain why they do what they do.**

- **Describe the effect their actions have on others in the scene.**

- **Explain why the actions are important in the play as a whole.**

Helpful connectives
- Briefly/to summarise/in short
- Because/the reason could be ... alternatively ... /possibly
- This causes/the effect is ... /this leads to/consequently/as a result
- This foreshadows ... /this act becomes significant ... /this is a turning point because ...

Grid 10 Planning a Shakespeare essay: the actions

Language

- **Pick out some key words in the scene and write about their meaning and significance.**

- **Explain the effect that Shakespeare might have wanted the words to have.**

- **Write about the atmosphere/tone that the words create.**

Helpful connectives
- This word relates to a major theme of the scene because . . . /however, the word can also imply that . . . /this phrase is important in the scene and in the play as a whole because . . .
- Shakespeare uses these images of violence to . . ./the author is asking the audience to consider . . ./Shakespeare uses wordplay at this point because . . .
- The atmosphere at this point is . . ./the author changes the tone here by . . ./the word . . . suggests . . .

Grid 11 Planning a Shakespeare essay: language used

Staging

- **Write about what you might see at certain moments, if you were watching a theatre performance.**

- **Write about the actions that an actor might perform when saying particular words or lines.**

- **Write about the effect that such actions might have on the audience.**

- **Explain how the director could achieve certain effects/build up the atmosphere by having the actors perform particular actions.**

Helpful connectives
- At this point, there could be . . . /the lighting could change here/if the actors were to . . . at this point, the action might suggest that . . .
- Lifting his hand up at this point, the actor could suggest . . . /the line could be emphasised if the actor were to . . . /the actor could either . . . or . . . at this point
- A pause here might suggest to the audience that . . . /saying the lines quietly might prompt the audience to wonder . . . /Shakespeare wanted the next action omitted from the play because . . .
- The director could ask the actors to . . . or (s)he could . . . /if the director . . . , the message would clearly be . . . /many alternative actions are possible here

Grid 12 Planning a Shakespeare essay: the staging

Also available...

🦌 **David Fulton** Publishers

How to Teach Fiction Writing at KS3
Neil Macrae

Using a step-by-step approach, based on the 'word/sentence/text level' convention, this practical manual shows how teachers can help pupils to build work in various genres and to move out from these to more complex writing. Each section has a workshop approach which leads into a narrative writing activity, giving pupils the chance to complete a fully realised piece of work at the end each time.

The workshops focus on:

* genre features
* the craft of the writer
* specific year-related needs (taken from the KS3 Framework)

£12.00 • Pb • 80 pages • 1-85346-858-4 • 2002

Grammar for Improving Writing and Reading in the Secondary School
Geoff Dean

Teachers can help their pupils become better readers, and write with greater confidence and control as a result of using the ideas in this book. The grammar knowledge being suggested, and the enjoyable contexts in which grammar can be learned, will bring about a greater degree of insight into texts, and should contribute to improved involvement in reading and writing for pupils of all abilities.

It includes:

* an important interpretation of KS3 English intentions
* advice on strong pupil involvement by making grammar learning fun
* a wider interpretation of the notions of 'framing' writing, more likely to support the literacy success of boys
* improved continuity of pupil study from KS2 to KS3.

£14.00 • Pb • 160 pages • 1-84312-003-8 • 2003

English Grammar and Teaching Strategies
Lifeline to Literacy
Joy Pollock and Elisabeth Waller

'extremely useful for teachers wishing to build their own knowledge - and as a basis for teaching whole class, small groups, children with special needs and children for whom English is a second language'

Junior Education

'In one hundred pages, this book provides just about everything you need to teach basic grammar' The book is very user friendly. It is clear and gives the right information and some excellent examples'

Hornsby Dyslexia Newsletter

Contents: Introduction - About this book; The need for grammar; The building blocks of grammar. Teaching strategies - general. Sentences; Nouns; Singular and plural; Articles; Adjectives; Verbs; Adverbs; Pronouns; Prepositions; Conjunctions; Phrases; Clauses; Speech; Punctuation; Paragraphs; Apostrophes; Figures of speech; Synonyms and antonyms; Homonyms, homophones and mnemonics; Conclusion.

£13.00 • Pb • 112 pages • 1-85346-638-7 • 1999

How to Teach Poetry Writing at KS3
Pie Corbett

This is a practical manual for teachers can be used directly in the classroom, and its suggestions include poetry games designed to warm up creativity and strengthen the imagination, followed by a series of creative poetry workshops which focus on developing a base of poetic techniques for young writers.

Workshops include:

* writing from first hand observation
* autobiography – valuing our lives
* writing about paintings, sculpture and music
* surreal boxes and the bag of words
* secrets, lies, wishes and dreams
* creating images, taking word snapshots
* riddles – hiding the truth
* red wheelbarrows and messages for mice

£12.00 • Pb • 80 pages • 1-85346-915-7 • 2002

Teaching English in the Key Stage 3 Literacy Strategy
A Practical Guide
Geoff Dean

'Geoff Dean has the gift of seeing English classrooms through teachers' eyes, uniting theory with practice in a way that leaves the reader hungry to try out his ideas.'

NATE

This book:

* interprets and explains for busy practitioners the National Literacy Strategy (NLS) document
* reinforces the messages of the NLS
* spells out the expectations of the framework and offers guidance on how to fulfil them
* describe and explains types of teaching methods to improve students' learning
* includes many practical ideas for classroom activities

£16.00 • Pb • 112 pages • 1-85346-860-6 • 2002

Literacy in the Secondary School
Edited by Maureen Lewis and David Wray

Based on the work of the influential Nuffield Extending Literacy Project, this book offers a range of practical suggestions for enhancing literacy work in the secondary school, building on foundations laid in the primary school by the National Literacy Strategy.

£16.00 • Pb • 192 pages • 1-85346-655-7 • 1999

David Fulton Publishers, The Chiswick Centre, 414 Chiswick High Road, London W4 5TF
Tel: 020 8996 3610   Fax: 020 8996 3622   E-mail: orders@fultonpublishers.co.uk
www.fultonpublishers.co.uk

To order...

 David Fulton Publishers

If you would like to order any of our books, or would like to request a copy of our complete catalogue, just photocopy this page and send it to:

David Fulton Publishers, The Chiswick Centre, 414 Chiswick High Road, London W4 5TF

Alternatively you can telephone, fax, email or order online:
Freecall: 0500 618052   Fax: 020 8996 3622
E-mail: orders@fultonpublishers.co.uk   on-line: www.fultonpublishers.co.uk

ORDER FORM

Qty	ISBN	Title	Price	Subtotal

Postage and Packing: £2.50 for one or two books.
Postage and packing is free for orders of three or more books.

P & P

Total

Payment

☐   By credit card (Visa / Access / Mastercard / American Express / Switch / Delta)

☐   By cheque with order. Please make cheques payable to David Fulton Publishers Ltd.

☐   With invoice (applicable to schools, LEAs and other institutions)

Credit card number ☐☐☐☐☐☐☐☐☐☐☐☐☐☐☐☐☐☐☐☐☐

Expiry date ☐☐☐☐ (Switch customers only)   Valid from ☐☐☐☐ Issue number ☐

Name	Order No./Ref
Position	Date
School/LEA/Company	
Address	
Postcode	
Telephone Number	Signature

"The details you are providing for this transaction will be used solely by the Granada Learning Group of companies and under the Data Protection Act 1998, will not be passed onto a third party. If you do not wish to receive any further product or promotional information from Granada Learning via either post or email then please tick the box below. If you have any queries regarding Granada Learning's use of your personal data then please contact "dataprotection@granada-learning.com"   ☐